Points of Depar

Six women rememb

Introductory and follow-on material: Jane Browne

Series editor: Angel Scott

Hutchinson / Virago

First published in Students' Virago in 1988 by Hutchinson Education and
Virago Press

Hutchinson Education
An imprint of Century Hutchinson Ltd
62–65 Chandos Place
London WC2N 4NW

Virago Press Limited
Centro House
20–23 Mandela Street
London NW1 0HQ

Century Hutchinson Australia Pty Ltd
89–91 Albion Street, Surry Hills,
New South Wales 2010, Australia

Century Hutchinson New Zealand Limited
PO Box 40–086, Glenfield, Auckland 10,
New Zealand

Century Hutchinson South Africa (Pty) Ltd
PO Box 337, Bergvlei, 2012 South Africa

Introductory and follow-on material © Jane Browne, 1988

Copyright © in each contribution held by the author 1988

Printed and bound by Richard Clay Ltd, Bungay, Suffolk

British Library Cataloguing in Publication Data
Points of departure.—(Students' Virago).
  1. Women – Biographies – Collections
  I. Browne, Jane
  920.72

ISBN 0–09–182343–9

Contents

The Students' Virago series

In the study of literature, readers are offered a bridge between themselves and the outside world: a chance to match their experience against that of other people. Books are an important part of the search for meaning and understanding. They introduce and reinforce the many different opportunities and possibilities open to us by presenting role-models and images that can help shape our lives. They also offer an area where we can recognise and embrace difference.

Most teachers and students today would accept that for books to fulfil this function, more work by women writers and more books about women and girls should be included in the curriculum. However, women's writing can differ from men's in content, genre and tone and there may be teachers and students who find it difficult to relate to some writing by and about women.

The Students Virago series aims to help put more women writers in the English curriculum:

- by careful selection of suitable titles from the extensive Virago lists
- by offering an introduction to the book that puts the writer and her work in context
- by offering a wide variety of follow-on activities to support the reading of the book.

The follow-on section of each book offers opportunities for working individually and collaboratively. The assignments are intended to suit the age-level at which the book may be studied and to meet the requirements of appropriate examinations. There are ideas for talking and writing about the book as well as ideas for extended study and wider reading.

Today, books by women writers, past and present, are attracting an ever-growing readership. This series aims to extend that readership even further by putting women writers in the English curriculum with books that we hope will be read and enjoyed by all.

Angel Scott

Introduction

This collection of autobiographical writing is about the process of remembering and understanding. Six very different women are featured here. Their childhoods were separated by time, country, social class and race. Yet each writer in turn, casting her mind back, brings together some of the places and people of her childhood. Each writer remembers too some of the experiences which were to shape her into an adult.

There is much humour here. The girls of these autobiographies are by no means 'little angels'.

- Kathleen Dayus, who grew up in great poverty in a back-to-back house in Birmingham, got up to all sorts of adventures with her sister and brother. With no form of entertainment provided for them, they made their own. Dressing up in Granny's long, black frock and using her bloomers to make a flag, they marched around the neighbourhood.

- Angela Rodaway, who grew up in Islington, London, knew the freedom of exploring with her brother. But one of their fishing expeditions took an unexpected turn when her catch of frogs escaped on a London bus and created havoc amongst the other passengers.

The surroundings of childhood evoke strong memories.

- Sita Devi, who grew up in Northern India, looks back with affection to village life there. She remembers happy times with friends and family before being sent to Britain to marry.

- Janina Bauman knew happiness too, in her early years with her family in Warsaw, Poland. But that happiness was to be shattered when Janina realised she was rejected by other people because she was Jewish. With the outbreak of the Second World War and the early triumphs of the Nazis, Janina's very life was at stake. Her courage and resilience show through in her writing.

This feeling of rejection is explored by other writers.

- Gail Lewis writes *From Deepest Kilburn*. Born of a British mother and Jamaican father, Gail knew the richness of two cultures at home. But children at school and on the streets of London abused and insulted her because she was black. Although deeply hurt by this experience of rejection, Gail learned to fight back.

Only one of the authors represented here made her living by writing.

- *As Once in May* looks back to a fragment of time and explores Antonia White's child's-eye view as a four-year-old. It is through those young eyes that we see some of the contrasts of Edwardian life with the 'downstairs' servants waiting on their 'upstairs' employers.

In the main these are ordinary women. Previously publishers would not have considered some of these lives important enough to record. It has needed the recent efforts of Virago – publishers of women's writing – to recognize the full significance of a whole range of ordinary lives.

Each writer spins her own individual thread of story, but considered together they weave a rich and diverse social fabric. As readers we are allowed a privileged glimpse into a range of fascinating lives.

Jane Browne

2

Her People
by Kathleen Dayus

About the author and the book

Her People is Kathleen Dayus' story of her childhood. Born in 1903, in Hockley, Birmingham, she grew up in real poverty, sharing three rooms with seven other members of her family. Their back-to-back house was so cramped that life spilled over into the communal yard of Camden Drive, shared by five families.

Kathleen describes the struggle her mother faced in keeping the family going through unemployment and hardship, a struggle that left her bitter and bad-tempered. Kathleen also tells with great humour of her exploits and adventures as an eight-year-old with her brother Frankie and sister Liza.

3

Our Yard

Our street was called Camden Street. Along one side of this street facing the high school wall ran ten terraces called 'groves'. Ours was called Camden Drive. There were five houses or hovels with five more back-to-backs to each terrace. They were all built the same; one large living-room, one bedroom, and an attic. There were also cellars that ran under each house, damp, dark and cold. Here was where they kept their coal, 'slack', or wood when they had any, which was never very often. For this reason there was usually some rubbish tipped in the cellar ready to be put on the fire for warmth or for cooking. I don't suppose this habit would be regarded as altogether healthy today but then it was essential.

Sometimes the shopkeeper down the next street would leave an orange-box with a few specked oranges left in it outside the shop, or a soap-box or perhaps a wet-fish-box. Then there would be a mad rush of us kids and many a fight would ensue as we dragged the box home for our parents to put on the fire. We'd skin away the mould on the oranges and share them out with those not lucky enough to grab a box.

My mum and dad slept in the main bedroom over the living-room and my brothers, Jonathan and Charlie, slept in another bed in the same room. My other brother, Francis or Frankie, and my sister, Liza, and I slept in the attic over the bedroom and my eldest sister, Mary, had her bed in the other corner of the attic facing ours. Mary was twenty and was going to be married soon, when she was twenty-one. She had to wait because Mum and Dad would not give their consent until she was of age. In 1911 my brother Jonathan (Jack) was nineteen and Charlie was eighteen, Liza was eleven, Frankie was ten and I was eight years old. Us younger ones slept three in a bed; Liza and I at the top and Frankie at the bottom.

One night I asked Mary if I could sleep with her in the

5

big bed but she told me, 'No! It's for me bottom drawers.' Now this puzzled me somewhat because I couldn't see how she could get a big bed like that in her bottom drawers.

We all lived in the first house in the fifth 'grove' which we all called 'our yard'. Next door lived Mr and Mrs Buckley and their six boys and one girl. In the third house lived Mr and Mrs Huggett with ten children: five boys and five girls. Next door to the Huggetts lived Maggie and Billie Bumpham. They had no children, or none that I knew of anyway. The neighbours used to say they weren't married and I could never understand this because I used to watch them undress and get into bed together – they never drew their blinds because they had none. What they did have that I loved was a little bull-terrier called Rags. Mrs Taylor lived in the last house in our yard. She had seven children and as many cats of both sexes who were continually producing offspring of their own: Mrs Taylor gave them to neighbours who needed them, to eat or clear away the mice. Everybody in our district had plenty of these. What she couldn't give away she drowned in the maiding-tub. No one knew what had become of Mr Taylor. Some people said she was so expert in drowning cats that she must have drowned him too.

At the end of the yard stood three ashcans and five lavatories, or closets as we called them. These each consisted of a square box with large round hole in the middle. Us children had to hold the sides of the seat otherwise we could have fallen in. These were dry closets. You can imagine the stench in summer! Next to the closets were two wash-houses where every washday everybody did their weekly wash. Like all the outhouses they were shared between the five houses in our yard and the five that backed on to us. There were always rows over whose turn it was to clean the closets so to save further quarrels Dad put a big padlock on one and gave

Mrs Buckley next door a key to share. We kept our key on a cotton-reel tied with string behind our living-room door. The other closets were left open for anyone to use and they were filthy. We had to hold our noses as we passed by, but Mum and Mrs Buckley always saw to it that ours was kept clean: her girls and Liza and I had to do it in turns while the women looked on. Finally, there was a gas-lamp in the centre of the yard and also a tap where everybody got their water for all household uses.

No one had a garden, not a blade of grass. There were cobblestones everywhere. If we wanted to see any flowers we went to the churchyard to play. We were often sent there, out of the way of our parents. We would take a bottle of tea and some milk for the younger ones who were transported in our go-cart. We nicknamed the churchyard 'Titty-bottle Park', a name that stuck with us for years. We'd tie the go-cart to a tree or a tombstone and play at hide-and-seek or perhaps some of us would change the stale water in the jam jars and rearrange the flowers. We'd be happy for a while playing at our games until the vicar appeared with his stick to chase us away. But try as he might he could never get rid of us; we always returned the next day.

All our homes were in old buildings that were tumbling down. The rent was usually three shillings a week; that was when the landlord was lucky enough to be paid. I've seen him wait until his tenants came out of the pubs at eleven at night. Often he wasted his time and if they couldn't pay their arrears he'd send along the bailiffs, but as often as not they'd already done a 'moonlight flit'. Down the street some one would borrow a hand cart, on the chattels would go and into another house they would move, for empty houses were common at that time. They were still the same old sort of hovel, though. The landlord rarely did any repairs, as the reader can imagine. So people did their own after their own fashion. When Christmas was drawing close they scraped together a few pence to buy some fresh wallpaper to brighten up the walls. I remember Dad used to paste ours with a mixture of flour and water and when Mum wasn't watching he'd mix in a bit of condensed milk. He swore it stuck the paper better but Jack said it only gave the bugs a good meal. Dad never stripped the old paper off. 'I daren't. It's only the bugs and the paper that's holding the walls up.'

They were dirty old houses; everyone had vermin or insects of some description. There were fleas, bugs, rats, mice and cockroaches – you name it, we had it. But I'll still say this for our mum; although we were as poor as the rest, she always kept us clean. Many times we had to stay in bed while she took the clothes from us to wash and dry in front of the fire so that we could go to school the next day looking clean.

Our mum was also very cruel and spiteful towards us, especially to me, and I could never make out why until I was old enough to be told. I can picture her now as I write. She was a large, handsome woman, except in her ugly moods. She weighed about sixteen stone and always wore a black alpaca frock, green with age, which reached down to her ankles, and a black apron on top. On her feet she wore button-up boots, size eight, which it was my job to clean and fasten with a steel button hook that hung by the fireplace. Mum always pretended she couldn't bend when she wanted her boots buttoned. She had long, black hair which she was always brushing and combing. She twisted it round her hand and swung it into a bun on top of her head. Then she'd look in the mirror and plunge a long hatpin through the bun. She called this hatpin her 'weapon'. Sometimes when she went out she'd put Dad's cap on top which made her look taller. She was always on the go, one way or another. I felt sorry for her at times and I tried my best to love her but we all lived in fear when she started to shout. When she did start you knew it. You had to move

8

quickly, for it was no sooner the word than the blow!

Many a time we felt the flat of her hand, Liza, Frankie and me. We never knew what for at times, but down would come the cane from its place on the wall. If we tried to run away then we really had it. Neither our parents nor the neighbours had any time to give us any love or affection and they didn't listen to our troubles. We were little drudges and always in the way. You may ask who was to blame for us growing up like this in squalor, poverty and ignorance. We were too young to understand why then, and I don't think I understand yet, but there it was, we had to make the best of it. My dad would listen to us sometimes but only when Mum wasn't about, or if he'd had an extra drop of beer. It was at these times that I liked him best because sometimes, not always, he was jolly. This wasn't very often because he was out of work, and had only Mum or his pals to rely on to buy him a drink. He had to do an odd job or two before Mum gave him his beer money. Sometimes he did odd jobs for other people on the sly, before the relief officer made his visit.

Our dad never hit us. He would tell us off and show us the strap but he left the correcting to Mum, and she did enough for both. So we young ones tried very hard to behave ourselves when Dad was out and he was more times out than in. He always said he couldn't stand her 'tantrums' but my brother Jack took over when Dad was out, pushing us this way then that and giving us the occasional back-hander if we didn't do what he told us.

We saw very little of my brother Charlie; he only came home to sleep. Mother's tantrums got on his nerves also.

Frankie and I were the best of pals. He always tried to get me out of trouble, but he often got me into some. But I still loved him.

My sister Liza was very spiteful to me as well as being artful and although I tried to love her she pushed me away and pinched me on the sly when she had the

9

chance. I couldn't do much about this because she was bigger than I was and very fat besides. When she did give me a sly dig I just had to grin and bear it and keep out of her and Mum's way. I still had to sleep with Liza and if she didn't pinch me she'd kick me out of bed. It was no good complaining, because Liza was always telling lies and Mum would believe her: she couldn't do wrong in Mum's eyes.

I remember one night very clearly. It was about one o'clock in the morning. I woke very thirsty so I crept quietly out of bed so as not to wake Liza or Frankie and went downstairs to get a drink of water. There wasn't any in the house, only a drop of warm water in the kettle. After satisfying my thirst I tiptoed back upstairs but when I got halfway up I heard Mum say, 'No! You can put it away! I've already had a baker's dozen. I'm 'avin' no mower so yow can get to sleep!'

I was always a very inquisitive child so I sat on the stairs to listen for more but I only heard the bed creak, so off up to the attic I went. I was feeling cold in my torn and threadbare chemise, one of Mary's cutdowns. I lay awake that night trying to puzzle out what my mum meant. I thought maybe she had eaten too much and wasn't feeling well so next morning when I came downstairs I said, 'Don't you feel well, Mum . . . have you eaten too much?'

At once she glared down at me and shouted, 'What do yer mean . . . 'ave I eaten too much?'

'Well, I heard you say to Dad you'd already had a baker's dozen,' I answered, trembling a little.

Mum went red in the face and cried out, 'And where did yer 'ear that?'

Then timidly I explained how I came down the stairs for a drink of water but before I could finish she slapped me across the face and shouted, 'That'll teach yer ter sit listenin' on the stairs!'

I moved back quickly as she lifted her hand once again

so I was quite surprised when she seemed to have second thoughts.

'I'll get yer dad ter settle with yow.'

Whether she told him or not I never found out but I was determined to find out one way or another what was meant by a baker's dozen. So that same night I waited for Mary to come up to bed and after Liza and Frankie fell asleep I crept over to her bed.

'Are you awake, Mary?' I whispered in the dark.

'Yes. What do yer want?' she snapped. She didn't usually snap at me, but I could see why she didn't want to be bothered at that time of night. I began to tiptoe back to bed when she lit the candle and called me.

'Come on, Katie. What is it you want?' she asked more pleasantly.

Just then Mum shouted up the attic stairs. 'Let's 'ave less noise up theea!'

Mary smiled as she put her finger to her lips. 'Hush,' she whispered. 'Come and get into bed beside me and get warm then you can tell me all about it.'

I snuggled up close and felt very comforted. I could have gone straight off to sleep, but Mary wanted to know what was troubling me.

'Can you tell me what a baker's dozen is, Mary?' I managed to ask between yawns.

'Why? Where did you hear that?' She sat up in bed looking at me quizzically, and as I told her a broad smile spread across her face.

'You were lucky to get away with only your face slapped.' I was wide awake by now.

'Well, what does it mean?'

'It means Mum didn't want Dad to love her and to have any more babies. She's already had thirteen which is what's called a "baker's dozen" and you being the thirteenth, Mum calls you the "scraping of the pot".'

I could still see her smiling in the candlelight as she

whispered to herself, 'I must tell Albert about this when we meet.'

'But if I'm the last, what became of the others in between?'

'They all died before you were ever thought of,' she answered sadly. 'Now lie down and go to sleep.'

We both snuggled up to keep warm after she blew out the candle. Although I was warm and comfortable I couldn't help but think about those other seven who had died. Maybe they were happier in the other world, I thought. There wouldn't have been room for them here, and Mum and Dad wouldn't have been able to feed us all. And with all these thoughts in my mind I eventually dropped off to sleep.

The Pig's Pudding

All the poor children in our school were provided with a breakfast, so when the bell rang out at five minutes to nine we had to be ready and waiting. The kids from our yard would rush up the street like a lot of ants because if you were not in line when the bell stopped you would be lucky to get any at all. The breakfast consisted of an enamel mug of cocoa and two thick slices of bread and jam. The bread was usually stale or soggy. Dad would get up very early some mornings and earn himself a few extra pennies fetching the big urn which contained the cocoa, and the bread and jam. He had to wheel it along to the school in a basket carriage and when he passed our yard Mum would be waiting with a quart jug hidden underneath her apron. When she could see no one about, Dad used to fill it with cocoa. She would have helped herself to the bread and jam too but Dad stopped her because they were all counted. Mum and Dad would have been in trouble with the authorities if they'd ever

12

been found out; but they never were. Our parents were both too cute to be caught, and although I knew what they were up to I never told anyone. I was too afraid in case they were sent to prison.

One morning we were dashing up the lane to get there in time for breakfast but the bell stopped ringing. Frankie grabbed my hand and dragged me along.

'Come on! We can still make it, Katie!' But I started to cry.

'We're too late now and I'm hungry!'

We hadn't had anything to eat since tea-time the day before, and then only a piece of bread and dripping.

'Shut yer blarting!' Liza hissed as she pushed us inside the door. Our teacher was calling the last name from the register when she saw us come in.

'I see you three are late again. I'm afraid you are too late for your breakfasts.'

'But we're hungry, miss!' pleaded Frankie.

'Well you can stand at the back of the line. You may be lucky,' she answered sharply.

We reached down a mug each from the ledge but when it came to our turn all we had was some warm cocoa, watered down, but no bread and jam. There was none left, and by the time our lessons were over at twelve o'clock we were very, very hungry.

On our way home from school we had to pass a homemade cook shop where we always paused to look through the window at all the nice things on show. This particular morning we stayed longer than usual, pressing our noses to the pane of glass, saliva dripping down our chins. There was pig's pudding, hot meat pies, hocks, tripe and cakes of every sort staring back at us. Worse than the sight of this potential feast was the smell. It was too much for Frankie who burst out: 'I'm so hungry I could smash the glass in and help myself.'

'And me!' I said.

'Don't you dare,' said Liza, who was afraid he would.

'Well, why should they be on show when we're so hungry?' asked Frankie.

Liza had no answer; she too was dribbling down her chin and she didn't stop Frankie who glanced quickly up and down the street to see who was about and hissed: 'If you two look out for me and as soon as "Skinny Legs" goes around the back of the shop I'll nip in quick and help myself to a few.'

Every one called the shopkeeper this because he gave short measure and he never gave you a stale bake or a loaf like other shops did. Anyway, it seemed ages before Frankie did anything but at last he saw "Skinny Legs" go through to the back of the shop and he dived in whilst Liza and I watched the street to warn him if anyone came along. I saw his hand in the window as he grabbed hold of a roll of pig's pudding and several hot meat pies. He came out, stuffing them under his gansey,* and the three of us ran off down the street as fast as we could but before we had gone many yards Frankie stopped.

'Catch hold of these pies, Liza, they're burning my belly!'

'No,' she replied, 'I don't want any part of them!'

'No? But you'll take your share to eat 'em, won't you!' he snapped.

I was sure someone would come along and overhear us so I put my hands up his gansey and pulled down the pies. He wasn't kidding, they were hot, but my hands were so cold I was glad of the warmth.

'Did anyone see me?' he asked anxiously.

'Yes. He did.' Liza was pointing at Jonesy, one of the lads from our yard.

'Hello, how long have you been there?' said Frankie.

'Long enough, and I seen what yer been dooin' an' all, an' if yer don't give me some I'll snitch on yer.'

---

*A corruption of 'guernsey', originally a fisherman's woollen jumper, but meaning here any thick, woollen sweater with a round or slit neck.

We all knew he meant it, so reluctantly Frankie pulled down the roll of pudding from his gansey and handed it over to Jonesy who dashed off home after saying he wouldn't tell anyone. But I knew he'd snitch all right. His mum went out cleaning on a Tuesday, so thinking she wouldn't be at home and he'd enjoy himself with his pudding he ran indoors. However he was unlucky: she was there.

'Where ever 'ave yer 'ad that from?' we heard her shout.

We heard his cringing explanation and Frankie shouted in the door, 'Yer traitor.'

Then the three of us ran down the yard to the wash-house to eat our pies. I don't think I ever tasted anything like that meat pie. It was delicious. Afterwards as we came from the wash-house we saw Mrs Jones walking towards our house. We knew we were in trouble but we didn't care now that our appetites were satisfied. Mrs Jones didn't like our mum, in fact I don't know who did, so I wasn't surprised by what happened next. Mrs Jones knocked loudly on our door and Mum lifted the corner of the curtain to see who was there. Seeing Mrs Jones she opened wide the door and shouted for all to hear, 'What do yow want?'

Mrs Jones stood on the step with her hands on her hips, grinning like a Cheshire cat. She always liked to get a dig at Mum, so she shouted louder so the neighbours could hear. 'I've got news for you, Polly. Your kids 'ave pinched some of "Skinny legs" ' pies.'

She didn't mention the pig's pudding though.

'I don't believe yer and get away from my dower, the lot on yer! Goo an' look after yer own kids.' And Mum slammed the door shut.

I thought, one day the door is going to fall off.

When Mrs Jones had gone away she came out again to call us in. Mrs Jones was still gossiping with the others.

'Come in, yow three. I want some explainin'.'

We went in timidly, but before we could utter a word she began angrily, 'An' what's this I 'ear about some pies?'

Liza quickly unburdened herself about how Frankie had stolen the pies and the pig's pudding.

'Pig's pudding. She never said anything about any pig's pudding.' She was furious.

'Frankie gave it to Jonesy,' said Liza.

'Well, we'll see about that!' said Mum.

She was fuming. She couldn't get out of the house quick enough. On went Dad's cap, off came the apron, and round the backyard she marched. When she got to Mrs Jones's door she banged twice, as hard as she could. All of the neighbours lifted their windows and popped their heads out while some of them crowded round to watch developments more closely. They knew Mum was big enough to eat Mrs Jones. There was no answer so she knocked again, louder and shouted, 'Yow can come out. I've seen yer be'ind the curtin.'

Slowly, Mrs Jones opened the door a little way to face Mum standing there, hands on hips, chest puffed out.

'Yer crafty old sod! Yow never told me that my Frankie giv' your lad a roll of pig's pudding. Now what about it? An' I ain't gooin' from 'ere till I get it.'

Mrs Jones was scared now, thinking what Mum might do, so she shut the door quickly and we all heard the bolt rammed home. But Mum wasn't finished. She banged again, louder than ever.

'Yer better 'and over that puddin' or else!' demanded Mum, her fist in the air.

Then suddenly the window shot up and the pig's pudding came flying out. It caught Mum on the head and everyone began laughing, but Mum ignored them and grabbed hold of us and the pudding and marched us indoors. She never bothered about what the neighbours thought or said as long as she didn't hear them. Woe betide them if she did.

'Get yer clo's off and get up them stairs. I'll get yer dad ter deal with you two when 'e comes 'ome.'

She pushed us towards the stairs and Frankie and I ran quickly up to the attic. We didn't go back to school that afternoon because Mum kept us up there until Dad returned in the evening and all we had to eat that day was the meat pie each.

It was late when we heard Dad come up the stairs so we pretended to be asleep. We knew he wouldn't wake us. Sure enough we soon heard his receding footsteps on the stairs. In the early hours of the morning Frankie crept downstairs and brought a cup of water and a thick slice of bread and lard. We shared this between us while Liza slept on. Then we climbed back into bed and finally fell asleep.

Christmas 1911

When Christmas came, Frankie, Liza and I went into the 'better' district which was not far from our school where there was a pub called the George and Dragon. This was a large public house with a long mixed bar, a gentleman's smoke-room, a bottle and jug department, and a 'snug' for ladies only.

We all knew when Dad went there to have a drink with his mates because I always had the job of pressing his best suit and his white muffler. When Mum went there with any of the neighbours she always wore her Sunday best, a stiffly starched pinafore which she took great pride in ironing, especially the lace edges. Her hair would be plaited round over each ear, instead of the usual bun on top. She always tried to make an impression. I can remember her saying, 'We're as good as this lot 'ere, even if we ain't got much.' The kind of people Mum was talking about were mostly shopkeepers and independent, but the folk who lived in our district were happier in their own little local, the Golden Cup. They used to say, 'We feel at home here; the gaffer and the missus are like us.' How true that was: they both drank like fish too! Their moods were unpredictable, though. They would sometimes join in with their customers and sing, or alternatively throw them out if they'd had enough. This usually happened on Saturday night when a burly, punch-drunk barman was employed for the purpose. Then there'd be a free-for-all – spittoons and sawdust flying everywhere. You never saw a pub empty so quickly as when someone peeped round the door and warned them that the cops were on their way.

The night before this particular Christmas Eve it was snowing and freezing hard when Frankie, Liza and I hurried along the street to sing carols. The shopkeepers were busy in their windows putting up their decorations ready for the Christmas spree. While this was going on, Frankie nipped smartly up the baker's entry and helped himself to a large, empty flour sack. This was to keep us warm while we waited for the shops to close and the pub across the street to fill with customers. The three of us sat on an empty shop step, huddled up close together with the sack over our heads to keep us warm. Although we were covered in flour we didn't mind as long as we didn't feel the cold. I was lucky; being the smallest, I sat between Frankie and Liza. Even so, my feet were cold and wet because my clogs were split at the sides and my clothes were threadbare.

At last we saw the lights go out in the shop windows. The street was deserted and dark now except for the lights that shone from the leaded windows of the George and Dragon, the knight in his brightly coloured armour making red, blue, green and yellow lights that glistened on the snow. We were just about to cross the street when we saw two shadows coming towards us. Quickly we dashed back to our hiding-place, but it was too late. Before we could hide our heads underneath the sack again, a man's hand dragged it from us. He struck a match and peered down at us.

'Well, well, well and what have we here? Three little orphans of the storm?' he chuckled.

We were too scared to move. We just sat there looking up at him wide-eyed. He called back over his shoulder, 'Aggie, is there any port left in the bottle?'

Aggie brought the bottle and said, 'It's time they were in bed and dreaming about Father Christmas.'

'Here, drink this.' He offered the port. 'It'll warm yer up.'

Frankie quickly took the bottle. I thought he was going to drink the lot but he gave Liza and me the bottle, and between us we finished the rest. There was only a drop for each of us which was a good thing because otherwise we'd have been tiddly. Anyway I felt warmer. Frankie gave him back the empty bottle after draining the dregs and saluted him gratefully.

'Thank you, sir. And a merry Christmas.'

The man put his hand into his waistcoat pocket and pulled out three pennies which he dropped in my lap.

'Do you want us to sing some carols?' I asked, hoping to return his kindness.

'Don't be silly; of course he don't!' said Frankie, giving me a nudge which nearly pushed me off the step.

His lady companion walked away as the man warned us to get off home before a bobby came along. But we had no intention of doing that.

'We ain't sat on this wet step just to go back home,' muttered Frankie.

So we pulled ourselves up off the step and walked a little way to hide in a doorway until they were out of sight. Then we dashed back to sing outside the George and Dragon. We were happy to have threepence and grateful for the port wine. It gave us Dutch courage. We could've faced anybody or anything that night, we felt so happy and warm inside. The other kids at our school

19

never sang carols here, they weren't allowed to go near this pub. Their parents used to frighten them by saying the owners were wicked people who, just like George and the dragon and the Mormons who came along our street, carried little children off. I asked Frankie if it was true about the Mormons.

'You don't want to believe everything people say. Anyway, our parents don't want us, yet they don't want the Mormons to have us either. It don't make any sense to me.'

'Shut up!' spat Liza. 'Let's get on with the carols. It's getting late.'

We stood just inside the doorway out of the snow, wiped the snow and flour off our faces, and began to sing. But we couldn't hear ourselves above the noise of merriment going on inside, so Frankie pushed open the door a little and kept his foot there. We waited until the sound had died down, then we burst with 'Hark, the Herald Angels Sing'. We sang at the top of our voices to drown Liza who was off-key as usual. Then someone shouted from inside, 'Some bloody angels!'

'Close the door,' somebody else cried.

This dampened our spirits. Frankie retrieved his foot and we walked away. However, before we'd got out into the street a kindly little lady came up behind us and gave us a silver sixpence. She told us to return on Christmas Eve, then she popped back inside, leaving us dumb-founded.

'Who was she?' asked Frankie.

'She's George's dragon we've heard so much about,' said Liza.

I was a bit disappointed. I'd imagined her to be a large woman something like our mum. We were happy, though. We ran to the fish shop to buy a pennyworth of fish and chips which we thought was plenty to share between the three of us. We ate it as we walked slowly back home. When we arrived, Frankie ran straight upstairs and put the rest of the money in a tin box which served as our savings bank. He had a good hiding-place, no one knew where, not even Mum.

The table was strewn with coloured papers which Mum had left for us to make our paper trimmings that night. We cut them all into loops and Liza made the paste with flour and water. If this failed, Frankie said he would get a tin of condensed milk to mix it with. Frankie took a little, not enough for Mum to notice, and this did the trick, and it was nice to lick our fingers each time we stuck one loop inside another and so we made the decorations for the walls and pictures. We didn't have a real Christmas tree. We had to beg two wooden hoops off a cheese tub from the grocer's. We fitted these one inside the other and covered them with different coloured tissue and crepe paper.

When Dad came home he said we'd done a good job and helped us hang the streamers across the room, high up above the clothes line: and to let people see we had some sort of tree, the paper Christmas tree was hung in the window from a nail. Every time we had a farthing or a halfpenny given us for running errands we bought white sugar mice and little chocolate Father Christmases and shiny, coloured balls and tinsel or any little thing we could afford. After we'd trimmed up the room, Dad gave us a penny each to buy extra gifts for the tree. Then, after drinking our cocoa, we went off to bed, happy and contented, knowing we had some money to spend and that we were going carol-singing again the next night to earn some more. We got up early in the morning to do our errands and daily chores around the house, then when it got dark we got ready to go out to continue our carolling. Mum watched us with keen eyes as we donned our coats and scarves.

'And where do yer think you three are gooin' this time o' night?' she asked sternly.

'We're going carol-singing,' Frankie replied, defiantly.

'That's all right,' Dad said, 'but be back in bed before we get home.'

'Yes, Dad,' we replied in unison.

We ran out and turned up the street towards the George and Dragon. I was glad Mum and Dad hadn't asked what part we were going to because this street was forbidden territory. When we arrived we started 'Hark, the Herald Angels Sing' again, but we only got as far as 'Hark' when I felt a hard thump on my back.

'Don't sing that one,' Frankie said. 'You know what happened last time. Let's sing 'Noël'.

Halfpennies and pennies came flying through the door and when I picked them up I counted tenpence ha'penny in all. We showed our gratitude by singing it again, only louder. But when Liza reached the high notes she gave an off-key shriek which brought George out with the warning to 'clear off'. Frankie turned on Liza as we walked away.

'You spoil everything with yer cracked voice. I wish I'd brought one of Mum's gob-stoppers along for you!'

She walked on, but never answered. We turned into our street where we thought we'd try our luck again. When we got to the Golden Cup, Frankie warned Liza to keep her mouth shut and pick up the money instead. We were unlucky this time, though. While we'd been up the street the other kids had been here, so we sang in vain. Next we tried the Mermaid, then the King's Head, but they told us the Salvation Army band had already called. We were reduced to singing for the passers-by, a few of whom gave us a penny. By now it was getting late and we remembered we had to be in bed before our parents returned, but we decided to satisfy our hunger first. We went to the cow heel and tripe shop and bought three pig's trotters. Frankie hid the rest of our earnings while we sat munching away. Then suddenly I remembered that Mum had told me that morning to mend a hole in my stocking.

'Don't forget to sew that 'ole or Father Christmas will leave yer nothin',' she'd said.

But I was too tired now. Anyway, I thought, perhaps she'll forget about it.

'Ain't yer going to hang up yer stocking?' asked Frankie as we were undressing.

'In a minute,' I yawned.

'Never mind. I'll hang it up,' he said, as I climbed into bed. Liza and I watched him hang three stockings over the bedstead. Then he jumped into bed and after blowing out the candle we fell to sleep.

Next morning we woke early and wished each other 'Merry Christmas' before looking to see what we'd been given. Liza jumped off the bed and grabbed her stocking while Frankie looked to see what was inside ours. Liza had an apple, an orange, some mixed nuts and a bright new penny. Frankie had the same, but when I looked in mine there was nothing, only the hole. In the dark Frankie had hung up the wrong stocking.

'Never mind.' Frankie was trying to be sympathetic and wiped my tears away. 'You can share mine.'

'But that's not the same. Mum's never loved me. I don't know why, Frankie, I always do as she tells me and I always try to please her,' I cried.

'Come and dry your eyes. It's Christmas Day. Anyway we've got our money-box hidden away for the holidays,' Frankie said cheerfully.

Liza didn't say a word. She was busy sucking her orange, sitting up in bed. So I sat up beside Frankie at the foot of the bed and he shared what he had with me. He nudged, winked and smiled at me with his big blue eyes. Then I returned his smile because his mirth was infectious.

This was the one morning in the year we had to stay in bed until Mum called us downstairs. So after eating our Christmas fare we got back under the bedclothes to keep warm, planning what we were going to do with our savings. All of as sudden we were startled by Mum's voice.

'Yer can get up now!'

We dressed quickly and went downstairs. Mary, Jack, Dad and Charlie were sitting at the table ready for us to join them. Mum was standing over a big fire frying eggs, sausages and bacon in a big pan.

'Merry Christmas,' we called out to them all. They each returned the greeting except Mum. She turned round to face us and waved the fork at the bowl of water for us to get washed.

''Urry yerselves. We're waitin' to 'ave our breakfast.'

After falling over each other to get to the bowl first, we sat down in our usual places on the sofa which was drawn up to the table. Dad, Jack, Mary and Charlie each had an egg, two sausages and a rasher of bacon. On our enamel plates was half a sausage, half an egg and a piece of fried bread. By the side of my plate was a small packet wrapped in tissue paper. I smiled across at Mum. I thought, she's not forgotten me after all.

'Thank you, Mum,' I said as I opened it.

She didn't turn an eye, only said, 'Yer can look at it when you've 'ad yer breakfast.'

I didn't want any breakfast, I was too anxious to see what was in the small packet. So while Mum wasn't looking I slipped my fried bread and sausage under the table to Frankie. Then I finished my half egg but I daren't leave the table until everyone else had finished. I looked at Mum and smiled.

'Can I please open it now, Mum?'

She didn't answer, so I presumed she meant me to and I eagerly unwrapped it and dropped the paper on the floor. It was a matchbox but when I opened it and saw what was in it I burst into tears. Inside was a little ball of black wool and a darning needle. I stared hard at it. My sister Mary came round the table and picked it up.

'How could you do such a thing to her?' she said. 'What's the reason?'

All eyes were on Mum now as I blubbered.

'That's 'er punishment fer not doin' as she was told!' Mum answered sharply.

Then Mary and Mum started to quarrel, and between my sobs I heard Mary accuse Mum.

'You've never loved her. But she'll know why some day!'

Mum walked over to the fireplace and Dad joined in.

'Now, Mary, let's have no more of this. It's Christmas Day, remember?'

Jack went out and Charlie followed behind him, banging the front door behind him. Dad patted me on the head and said softly, 'I'll be back when you've settled your arguments.' Then he too walked out.

Frankie and Liza just looked at Mum. I didn't know what they were thinking but I knew why she'd given me the needle and wool. I went upstairs and took off my stocking and began to darn it when Mary came in to see me. She unfastened her trunk and took out a box of lace handkerchiefs. 'Here you are, Katie,' she said. 'Here's my present for you.'

I thanked her with a sob and a smile.

'Don't take Mum to heart too much, Katie. She didn't mean anything.'

I knew she was making excuses for Mum. I knew Mum didn't love me from piecing together bits of conversations I'd overheard, and now this morning I'd heard Mary say so to Mum.

'Mary,' I asked as I put on my stocking, 'do you know why Mum doesn't love me?'

'She does, in her funny way,' she said gently.

'She can't do or she wouldn't do and say the things to me that she does. Won't you tell me why?' I sobbed.

'When you're older,' she said. Then she went downstairs.

'That's all I get off you grown-ups; "when yer get older",' I answered angrily, following her down.

Granny Moves In

Each Friday night Liza, Frankie and I had to stay up later than usual. This was not a treat, far from it. We had to blacklead the grate and the big, iron kettle that stood on the hob, as well as rub off any soot on the enamel teapot that stood beside it. On the other hob was a battered copper kettle which had a hole in the bottom; Mum never threw anything away. She said Dad would mend it one day, but he never did, and we still had to polish it. Jutting out from the top of the grate was a large meat jack which always held our stewpot. I called it a witch's cauldron. We had to scrub the deal-topped table, the stairs, chairs and broken flag-stones, brown as they were from years of hard wear. The soda we used hardly touched them, the only things that were cleaned were our hands.

Standing each side of the fireplace were two wooden armchairs, one for Mum and one for Dad. We children were never allowed to sit in these unless given permission to do so, but we did make good use of them when Mum and Dad were out at the pub. Our usual seat was the old horsehair sofa under the window. Someone had given this to Dad in return for doing odd jobs. It replaced the old wooden one which was chopped up for firewood. Only the legs were spared because Dad said they might come in handy for something one day. Every corner of the house was cluttered up with odds and ends. Our sofa was moulting badly and had bare patches all over. We nicknamed it 'Neddy'.

Beside the table were two ladder-backed chairs, one for my brother Jack and the other for Mary. There had been three but after Charlie and Dad had a row over money, Charlie left home, and Dad burnt the chair. There was also a three-legged stool under the table; on its top stood our large, tin washing bowl. Set into the wall beside the fireplace was a long, shallow, brown earthenware sink. We only used this for putting dirty crocks in because we had no running water indoors. On the other side of the fireplace was an alcove behind the stairs door where the old, rotten mangle was kept; this was a permanent fixture. We had orders that if anyone called we had to leave the stairs door open to hide our laundry from view.

The fireguard, round the fireplace, was always covered with things airing or drying, especially when the lines across the room were full. Around the mantel-shelf was a string fringe with faded, coloured bobbles and on the shelf were two white, cracked Staffordshire dogs and several odd vases which contained paper flowers and pawn tickets. Hanging high on the wall above was a large photograph of our granny. We'd have loved to have got rid of it, but didn't dare. When you stared at it, the eyes seemed to follow you round the room. The effect was heightened at night when the paraffin lamp was lit. This was the only picture in the room with the glass intact. Mum in particular objected to it.

'I carn't see why yer don't 'ave a smaller picture of 'er. It takes up too much room.'

'No!' Dad would reply. 'Nothing's big enough for my mother. It stays where it is.'

'It'll fall down, you'll see, one of these days!' Mum replied.

'Not if you don't intend it to. But I'm warning you, Polly!' He wagged his finger at her in admonishment. So there the picture stayed.

We also had to dust all the pictures and knick-knacks that hung over the walls. There were three pictures, 'Faith', 'Hope' and 'Charity', as well as a print of 'Bubbles' – the advertisement for Pear's soap – and many photographs of Mum's first-, second- and third-born, all dead and gone. Underneath these were the death cards and birth certificates of the others, and photographs of relatives framed in red and green plush.

They were so faded you had to squint to recognise who they were. There were even paper mottoes stuck to the wall which announced such sentiments as 'God Bless This House' and 'Home Sweet Home'. I could never understand why they were there, our house or home was far from happy. They were supposed to be Christmas decorations but they were not taken down until Easter, when Mum folded them up and put them away for next year.

On the wall opposite was a picture of Mum and Dad taken years ago on their wedding day. Mum looked happy, wearing leg o'mutton sleeves with her hair parted in the middle. She was smiling up at Dad who stood beside her chair. Dad had one hand on her shoulder and was standing erect like a regimental sergeant-major. His hair was dark like Mum's and was also parted in the middle, with a kiss-curl flat in the middle of his forehead. His moustache was waxed into curls at each end. He held a bowler across his chest. Now as it happened this was the very same hat which had pride of place on the wall, just low enough for me to dust. One night I happened to knock this hat on the floor just as Mary entered. As I stooped to retrieve it she said, 'You'd better put that back on its nail before Mum comes in.'

So I snatched it up and, as I put it back, I replied, 'It's no good. It's going green. About time Mum got rid of it, like most of the relics here.'

'You'd better not let Mum hear you. She happens to be very proud of that. It has a lot of memories for her.'

I went on working about the room; then I noticed that Mary was smiling. 'What are you smiling at, Mary?'

'Come and sit down and I'll tell you about it.'

I sat on 'Neddy', but before Mary sat down she peeped round the curtain to see if anyone was coming. Then she began her story.

'Now that billy-cock –' she pointed towards Dad's delapidated hat, '– that hat has sentimental value for

Mum. About the time when she started having the family . . . I'll tell you all about it, but only if you don't laugh and can keep a secret. Every twelve months Mum gave birth to a baby and when it was a few weeks old Mum and Dad went to church to have it christened. They thought they'd gone on their own. They never saw me watching them. I used to hide behind the pillar.'

Her face was beaming and I was intrigued to hear what was coming next.

'Now when the parson took the child off Mum he'd sprinkle water on its forehead and then it would cry and water would come out the other end. When the parson had finished the christening and handed Mum the baby she'd sit down in her pew and change its nappy. Well, it was then that Dad was at the ready. Taking off his billy-cock he'd take out a dry nappy and put the wet one inside the hat and then when he replaced it on his head, they'd leave the church and go in the pub to celebrate. You see I always followed them, just like you do.'

She gave me a sly wink and we both burst out laughing.

'Phew!' I cried, holding my nose.

Then she left and I finished my chores and although the house looked and smelt better it was not fresh air, it was carbolic soap and Keating's Powder. In the end I was almost too tired to crawl up the attic stairs and fall into bed. I just peeled off my clothes and was asleep immediately. I didn't even say my prayers.

Friday wasn't the only day I had chores to do. Saturday mornings was my day to get up early and be down to riddle the overnight ashes and place the embers in the steel fender ready to place on the back of the fire when it was lit. It was also my job to make a pot of tea and take a mug for Mum and Dad.

Now as the reader can imagine, Mum's temper wasn't always at its longest first thing in the morning. She'd yell at me, 'The tea's too 'ot!' or 'It's too cold!' or 'Not enough sugar in it. You ain't stirred it up!' She'd find fault with anything. This particular morning I was saved from her nagging, but only for a short time. Just as I was about to take the mug of hot tea upstairs, a loud knock sounded on the door. I lifted the corner of the curtain and peeped out. It was only the postman, who was a cheery man with a smile for everyone he met.

'Good morning, Katie, and how are you this bright, cheery morning?'

'Very well, thank you, Mr Postman,' I replied.

If only everybody in our district was as pleasant, life would have been much happier. He asked me to give a letter to Dad and returned down the yard. He'd only just stepped down from our door when Mum shouted, 'Who's that bangin' on the dower this time of the mornin'? Carn't we get any sleep around 'ere?'

She'd forgotten that she woke everybody, singing and banging at the maiding-tub at six o'clock every Monday morning.

'It's the postman, Mum. He's brought a letter for Dad,' I called back from the foot of the stairs.

I put the letter between my lips and turned to get the mugs of tea. It was then that I saw the postman standing under the window, shaking his head from side to side. I heard him tutting to himself as he walked down the yard. Mum shouted down again for the letter, so I hurried up to the bedroom where I found her sitting up in bed. I put the mugs down on the cracked, marble-topped washstand and had the letter snatched from my lips.

'An' about time too!'

'It's for Dad,' I said, loud enough to wake him.

'I know, I know' she repeated. 'An' where's me tea?'

'On the table,' I answered timidly.

I made to go downstairs, but she called me back to read the letter. Mum couldn't read or write. She couldn't even count, except on her fingers and then it always took a painfully long struggle. I always did any reading or writing when Dad wasn't about. Dad could correct my spelling because he was more literate than Mum and he spoke better too. I watched him stir and yawn as I fumbled with the envelope. I was glad he was awake; it was his letter anyway. But he waved me away.

'Oh, read it, Katie, and let's get back to sleep.'

I was anxious myself now to find out what the letter contained but when I'd opened it and read it there was no extra rest for anyone that morning. It was from Granny and although her spelling was bad I managed to read it out.

'"Sam an Polly,"' I read aloud, '"Im not well in elth me ouse as got ter be fumigated The Mans bin an ses Ive gotter move for two weeks so Im coming ter you Ill bring wot bitta money I got and Im goin ter joyn the salvashun army and Ill bring me rockin chare and me trunk so Ill see yer all tomorra so be up early. Hannah."'

She didn't ask if she could come, she just assumed she could. When I'd finished reading the jumbled and nearly illegible writing, Mum jumped up with a start.

'Good God above!' she cried, waving her arms about. 'We ain't 'avin' 'er nuisance agen, are we?'

She glared at Dad, who was still lying on his back. He wasn't asleep. Who could be, the way Mum was raving? But he did have his eyes closed. He was thinking about how to deal with Mum.

'Yow asleep, Sam? Dain't yer 'ear wot I said?'

'I heard yer,' he shouted back and opened his eyes wide. 'The whole bloody town can hear when you start.'

'Well, what can we do?

'It's only for two weeks. Nobody will take her, so we'll have to do the best we can,' Dad replied.

*

Very early next morning, before anyone was awake, I heard a loud knock on the downstairs door and before I could get out of bed a louder knock and three taps on the

31

window pane. I woke Frankie and Liza with a good hard shake and told them what was happening. We three got out of bed and dressed quickly. Then we lifted the window to see what the racket was all about. As we leant over the window sill to look down into the yard below we saw Granny at the door, calling and waving her arms in all directions.

'Ain't nobody awake yet! 'Ave I gotta stand 'ere all day? I'm freezin' an' if nobody lets me in I'm comin' through the winda.'

She sounds just like Mum, I thought. Then, before anyone could get down to let her in, she tried to push up the window. Turning to the little man who'd brought her things on a hand cart, she shouted for assistance. He looked too scared to move. Then Granny saw the bucket of rainwater that Mum kept for washing her hair. She promptly tipped the water away and turned the bucket upside down. Then she pushed the window up and stepped on to the bucket to aid her entry. The reader can imagine what a funny sight sixteen stone Granny was, standing on a rusty old bucket. We were not used to the capers that Granny cut. Suddenly, just as she was halfway through, disaster struck. The sash cord broke and the bucket slipped, leaving Granny pinned half in, half out, by the window frame. She began to kick her legs in a vain attempt to free herself but she only succeeded in showing the neighbours her pantaloons. For the first time we experienced a temper worse than Mum's. She swore till the air was blue. Proof, I thought, that she needed to join the Salvation Army. Then Dad popped his head out of the window and called down angrily, 'You'll have to wait, Mother, while I slip me trousers on.'

When he came downstairs and saw the plight she was in, he lifted the window but he was too quick. Granny fell out backwards, rolled over the bucket and landed in a puddle of rainwater.

'An' about time too,' she bawled while he struggled to pick her off the floor.

'I'll get meself up,' she muttered.

By this time Mum's head had appeared at the window and the neighbours too were peering down at the commotion.

''Annah!' Mum shouted. 'Yer'll wake up all the neighbours.'

'Wake 'em up! Wake 'em up!' she shrieked, struggling to her feet.

She turned round and waved her fist at the amused onlookers and bellowed at them, getting redder and redder in the process.

'Look at 'em! The nosy lot of idle sods.'

All the time she'd been carrying on, the little old chap was standing still, waiting to be paid for his labours. Suddenly she turned on him, leaned against the cart and sniffed.

'Don't stand there all day. 'Elp me off with me trunk an' me rockin'-chair. An' mind 'ow yer 'andle me aspidistra.'

He couldn't manage the trunk nor the rocking-chair, but Dad soon came to the rescue. Meantime Granny felt inside the bosom of her frock, sniffed a couple of times and pushed a silver sixpence into his outstretched hand. He looked down at it disdainfully and mumbled a barely audible 'Skinny old Jew.'

'What did yer say?'

'I said, "Thank you",' he answered meekly.

'Dain't sound much like "thank yer" ter me,' she retorted.

Scratching his head, he wheeled his empty cart away and said to Dad in a louder voice, 'I feel sorry for yow, mate,' but Dad ignored him.

The neighbours closed their windows. The fun was over for them but for us the trouble was only just beginning. We dressed hurriedly and dashed down to see Granny. She looked huge standing beside the trunk. We hadn't seen her for some time and it was easy to forget her size. She wore a black taffeta frock almost to her feet, black elastic-sided boots and a battered black woollen shawl. Her lace bonnet, also black, was hanging from ribbons on the back of her neck where it had slipped while she'd been trying to climb through the window. Her hair, too, was dishevelled, but what I noticed most was the large raised lump on her behind. I poked Frankie and he whispered, 'Ain't she got a big bum.'

'That ain't her bum. It's a bustle,' I replied as he started to snigger.

Liza too stared at Granny, but Granny paid us no attention until she suddenly straightened herself up to her full height of six feet, pulled her shawl around her and addressed us. 'Don't just stand theea gorpin'. Come an give yer ol' gran a kiss.'

I closed my eyes and lifted my face up sideways for her to kiss my cheek. She must have read my thoughts because she just pushed me roughly away, with a slap and bent to peck Liza and Frankie's cheeks. As I walked off clutching Topsey she asked what I was holding.

'It's the golly you made me, Granny,' I replied.

'I don't remember mekin' that.' She shrugged her shoulders and dismissed me.

'Now, now, Mother. You gave it to her last Christmas. You must have forgotten.' Dad attempted to pacify her.

'Er's always forgettin',' Mum piped up from putting Granny's plant away.

'Put the kettle on, Polly, and we'll all sit down and have a cup of tea.'

This was Dad's favourite tactic when he saw a quarrel brewing. He drew Gran's rocking-chair towards the fire. Granny sat down and rocked in the creaking chair. With hers in the middle and Mum's and Dad's chairs on either side of the fireplace no one else could feel or see the

34

flames. I picked up Topsey and sat with Frankie on 'Neddy' to await my tea. When it was made, Granny's was the first cup to be filled. Then she took a sip and without warning spat it back out.

'What yer call this?' she spluttered, pulling a face at Mum.

'It's yer tea. Like it or lump it.' This was a favourite retort.

'Tastes like maid's water* ter me.' Granny could give as good as she got.

We looked at each other; we all knew what Mum's tea was like. The pot had been stewing all morning. Dad told me to make a fresh pot. As I squeezed past Mum to empty the tea leaves into the spare bucket, I heard her whisper to Dad, 'Thank the Lord we've only got 'er fer two weeks.'

During Granny's stay the gas-fitters came to connect the place to the mains. We'd already had the enamelled iron stove and the gas mantle fixed to the wall weeks before. They'd also fitted a slot meter to the wall at the bottom of the broken cellar stairs. It was lovely to see the lighted gas mantle after the paraffin lamp. We still had to keep this relic, along with the others, in case Mum ran out of pennies. We also had to have a candle to light us to bed because, as Mum said, 'It's not safe to have gas upstairs.' I thought it was much more likely that she objected to gas in our bedrooms because she had candles free from Jack's works. He always brought a couple home in his pockets every night. He supplied Granny too. She didn't believe in having gas installed at all, and said, 'When I die I wanta goo ter me Maker in one piece, when me time comes!'

The following Saturday afternoon Mum said they

---

*Outmoded slang for wine.

were going to the Bull Ring* to do the shopping. This was our marketplace, where everything was sold cheap. There was the fruit and vegetable market, the fish market, the rag market and the flower market, all next to each other; and on each side of the street were barrow boys shouting their wares.

Dad asked Granny if she would like to go as well, but she said, no, that it was too noisy, and that there was too much swearing for her liking. I could tell by the look on Mum's face that she didn't want Granny to go but Dad asked anyway.

'No. I can find summat betta to do with me time. Anyway I'm gooin' ter see the Captain of the Salvation Army,' Gran replied when pressed.

'Come on, Sam, before she changes 'er mind,' Mum said irritably.

As he was leaving the house, Dad said, 'Now if you kids behave yourselves I'll bring yer back a little present from town.' Then off they went, slamming the door behind them.

'Things must be looking up,' said Frankie, 'Dad's getting generous.'

'Well,' I answered, 'he's better than Mum.'

'Perhaps.' He shrugged his shoulders.

Granny put on her bonnet and shawl and went off to the Salvation Army Hall without a word to us. We were at a loss for something to do: then our eyes alighted on Granny's trunk. Frankie heaved open the rusty tin lid and we peered eagerly inside to see what secrets it held. We were disappointed to find only a pair of white pantaloons, a long, black lace frock with a bustle, a pair of button-up boots and a pair of whalebone stays like

---

*The Bull Ring was the centuries-old daily marketplace. Nearby were the wholesale fruit and vegetable and fish markets. The old markets were demolished in the late 1960s and have been replaced by a new complex. The modern Bull Ring is an enormous covered shopping centre which straddles Birmingham's inner ring road.

Mum's. We lifted them out to see what was underneath. It was then that we discovered Granny had been in the Army before. There was a tambourine, a uniform, and a bonnet with a red ribbon with 'Salvation Army' written on it. Underneath these was a bundle of old papers tied with string. We were about to start returning these things to the trunk when I hit on an idea to amuse ourselves until the grown-ups returned.

'Let's dress up and pretend we're in the band,' I said. The other two agreed.

Frankie fetched Mum's broom handle and tied the pantaloons on to it to represent a flag. Liza put on the bonnet and carried the tambourine and I put on the long black frock with the bustle. When we were ready we marched up and down the yard. Frankie waved the flag, Liza banged the tambourine and I dragged the bustle behind me. We sang 'Onward, Christian Soldiers' as we marched back and forth. All the neighbours turned out to see what all the noise was about. They joined in too. People sang a lot in those days. The children joined our band and we paraded up and down. Frankie's pantaloons bellowed out in the breeze as Liza's tambourine kept the beat. We were having great fun until Liza gave one hell of a scream, dropped the tambourine and ran into the house. Frankie and I were scared stiff, thinking it was Granny or our parents come home early. Frankie dropped the broom and followed Liza into the house. I tripped over the long frock in my anxiety to follow them. Everybody was giggling, thinking it was all part of the act. When I did manage to get indoors I saw Liza was standing on 'Neddy' still screaming and pointing at the bonnet. We couldn't understand what she was screaming about until she flung the bonnet violently at Frankie. I stooped down to pick it up when I was startled by a mouse which suddenly ran out across the floor. Liza was still hysterical but Frankie and I tried to catch it; the mouse was too fast for us. Like a flash it ran down a hole under the stairs and was gone. We must have caused quite a commotion because people had gathered round our door to see what all the fuss was about. They disappeared quickly enough when I told them what it was though. I couldn't understand why they were so squeamish; they had plenty of mice of their own.

We managed to quieten Liza down eventually. Then we packed Granny's belongings back into the trunk, but we had a good look to see if we'd left any other little friends behind. Then we fastened down the lid just as we'd found it.

Now perhaps the reader will remember what I've written about Liza telling Mum tales about Frankie and me, so we warned her that if ever she said anything about what had happened we'd put the mouse down her frock while she was asleep. Liza knew that whatever Frankie said he meant, so she promised not to say a word. We'd only just put the things away and set the kettle on the stove when the door opened and Dad walked in.

'Yer been good kids?' were his first words.

Frankie said we had, and warned Liza with a look.

'Well, here you are.' Dad handed me a box. I couldn't believe my eyes when I opened it. There, sitting on some straw, was a tame white mouse with tiny pink eyes.

'Oh, it's lovely,' exclaimed Frankie.

'Thank you, Dad.' I was overjoyed, but Liza didn't look or speak. Frankie stared at her in a meaningful way and she said nothing.

'You're not to let it out of the cage,' Dad told us. 'We don't want any offspring. We've got enough already.'

'I don't know why yer bought it,' Mum snapped.

'I didn't buy it. It was given me,' Dad replied.

'Hm . . . hm . . .' She obviously didn't believe him. 'I've 'eard that before.'

Just at that point I opened the cage to stroke it. Liza gave an enormous scream when she saw, and jumped on a chair.

'Don't be a babby,' Dad told her. 'It ain't going to hurt yer.'

'It ain't going to get a chance,' she retorted, climbing gingerly down from the chair.

I really thought she'd tell Dad our secret now so, as Dad turned to the fire to light his pipe, Frankie whispered in her ear, 'I'm warning you. If you let on, this is the one I'll put down your neck.'

She went pale and we didn't hear another word from her for the rest of the day.

'Where shall we keep it?' asked Frankie.

'We'll keep it on the attic shelf, away from Pete,' I answered.

We asked Dad what sex it was, but he said he didn't know so we called it Snowy to be on the safe side. Each night before we went to bed we fed it on breadcrumbs we'd saved and watered it on cold tea in a cocoa-tin lid. Frankie and I were so proud of our little pet and we showed it to all the kids in the yard, but we didn't let them touch it. As the days went by, Snowy looked well and happy running up and down his cage, standing on his back legs or washing his face; until one morning when we went to give him his tea and crumbs the cage was no longer on the shelf. There was a scuffle on the floor and there we saw the cage with Snowy still inside and Pete trying to get his paw between the bars. I shouted in alarm to Frankie but before I could rescue the mouse a clog came flying across the room. Pete was not deterred by this though. He only retreated under the bed from where he watched, ready to pounce again if the opportunity offered. As I bent down to reach for the cage I caught Liza out of the corner of my eye grinning all over her face. She lay back quickly and hid under the bedclothes. Then I guessed how the cage came to be on the floor. Frankie had guessed, too. He snatched at the cover and dragged her out and accused her. He was just

39

about to strike her when we heard Mum's heavy tread on the stairs.

'What's all that racket and what yer all doin' out of bed?' she demanded. 'Get back, the three o' yer, before yer feel the back of me 'and!'

I crawled out from under the bed where I'd been keeping Pete at bay. Liza lay on the floor whimpering and although we tried to explain, Mum wouldn't listen. She made us bare our bottoms and slapped us hard and pushed us on to the bed. She seemed to have the strength of a tiger when she was roused. We were really scared and so was Snowy, who was running madly round inside his cage. We sat watching Mum nervously, wondering what she was going to do next. She struggled to get down on her knees to reach under the bed for the cat.

'Come on out. I know yer theea!'

But Pete sensibly stayed put. He was used to Mum's rough handling so he remained where he was hiding under our comics. However, after fumbling around she eventually managed to grab his tail. Then, as she tried to pull him out, we heard hissing and spitting. This had its effect on Mum who was afraid he would fly at her. So she let go and Pete, his fur standing on end, flew down the stairs. Mum heaved herself off the floor with considerable effort and, seeing Snowy's cage, she snatched it up.

'Not another word from any of yer!' she yelled, and with that marched downstairs.

We knew very well what Mum's temper was like and we were sure she'd get rid of the mouse. Without waiting to dress, Frankie and I ran down the stairs two at a time and peeped round the corner into the living-room. Mum was nowhere to be seen but there on the table was the cage with Snowy still tearing round inside it. Pete had also plucked up his courage to make another attempt to catch him and was sitting glaring at the mouse. We made a dash for the table but Mum must have loosened the catch because, when Pete clawed at the cage, the door flew open and like a flash Snowy fled down the same hole as Granny's mouse before either of us could grab him. I began to sob, but I stifled my crying when I saw Mum standing in the doorway. Silently she reached for the cane but we were saved from a thrashing when the door opened and Dad walked in. 'Now what's going on here?' he asked. 'What yer doing standing there in yer underclothes.'

We didn't get a chance to explain. Mum told the story her way and ended by pointing out the hole that our mouse had disappeared down. 'An' that's the larst of that,' she added. 'Yow never ought to 'ave bought it. I'll get rid of the cat as well, fer all the good 'e is.'

'All right. Calm down. Don't keep on about it. Anyway it'll be happy enough down there with the rest of them. And get back upstairs, you two, and put some clothes on before you catch yer death. Go on, GET!'

There was nothing else to do but obey, but as we climbed slowly up the steep flight Liza pushed past us on her way down, fully dressed.

'I'll pay you out for this, you wait and see,' Frankie hissed.

'It's all her fault,' Frankie grumbled as we were dressing.

I agreed with him, and tears began to trickle down my cheeks again.

'Even Granny pretends to be deaf when we tell her anything.' I nodded my agreement.

For weeks after, when nobody was about, we'd wait by that hole in the hope of catching a glimpse of our Snowy. We even pushed scraps into the hole so he wouldn't be hungry. Little did we know it was the worst thing we could have done. Still, we were happy knowing he would have Granny's mouse down there to play with. Each night I mentioned Snowy in my prayers and asked Jesus to watch over him because Frankie and I missed him so much.

41

Top: Number 1 Court, Camden Drive was identical in every respect to Number 4 Court where Kate's family lived. Five three floor, three-room back-to-back houses faced the communal toilets and wash houses, across the brick yard.

Bottom: This court at the rear of Holland Street was typical of thousands in the densely-populated central wards.

Top: The ground floor living room of a court house like Kate's. The sparse furnishings, small ornaments and pictures over the range are just as the author describes her own house.

Bottom: Black Country hop-pickers, Herefordshire, in 1896. Kate's family, like many others, would take working excursions into the countryside.

Kate's brother Charles holding his first-born son, Camden Street, 1922.

Kathleen Dayus in 1933.

Top: A view from the High Street looking towards St Martin's-in-the-Bull-ring as it was in 1895, with the market stalls in the shadow of the church.

Bottom: The heart of Joseph Chamberlain's remodelling of Birmingham was the Council house, seen on the left here. Colemore Row which stretches into the distance was cut through an area of poor housing and its inhabitants moved into areas like that Kate grew up in.

A London Childhood
by Angela Rodaway

About the author and the book

Angela Rodaway writes with humour and affection of her life growing up in Islington, London. Born in 1918, Angela grew up in poverty; her father was often unemployed and the family had to 'make do' in order to survive. Their crockery was throw-outs from a local pottery, their clothes were seconds, their food bought cheaply at closing time.

Despite all this, Angela's mother worked obsessively hard to ensure 'standards' were maintained, keeping the family on the narrow path between, in her words, 'slovenliness' and 'snobbishness'.

Angela's spirit of adventure often got her into scrapes and she writes of her memories with an eye for detail as well as for the amusing.

Less Humble Beginnings

I was seven years old in the year nineteen twenty-five and many things were different, then, from what they are now. Perhaps rich people were richer. Certainly the very poor were in greater numbers, and it was to the latter class that we belonged. We were never so ill-dressed that toes came bare through our broken shoes, but rarely were we so well shod that the naked soles of our feet did not touch the pavements as we walked.

Time is a dull line to string events on. Things count for more or less according to the thread that runs through them. Perhaps, though, the first memory is of first importance, in that it is supposed to indicate one's 'life style', one's key attitude to life, the essential situation which, in personal relationships, one constantly recreates. Mine puts me in a bad light straight away.

It is round about the time of my second birthday and there are the wooden bars of a cot, which had been made by my father. I am outside the cot, not in it. Through the bars and just on a level with my face is the head of a baby, with startled blue eyes, and his milk-white face is pursed voluptuously round the teat of his feeding-bottle. It is easy to take the bottle, through the bars, climb on to the prickly, dark green sofa, surrender to two minutes' utter bliss, then put the bottle back again, empty. The baby does not even cry. His face wears a look of hurt astonishment.

Later I adopted a maternal attitude towards this younger brother and used to 'mind' him, if we were left alone in the room. He had a soft, pale, pliant face and sometimes I would pull it about, stretching down his eyelids, pushing up his nose or pulling back his cheeks so that his mouth went wide, quite gently, not to hurt him, merely to make him look ugly, so that I could call our mother to look. On baking day, I made a 'baby' of my own and the dough felt just like my brother. When it was cooked it was not the same at all.

My father had iron-grey hair, short, curly and resilient, like a spade beard upside-down. His face was mahogany, his neck raw beef and his eyes were the washed blue of shadows on snow. He loved wild life and had lived in Canada for a long time. It was there that, one evening, his pet bull-dog had gone wild, leapt at him and clung to his upper lip, until the flesh tore. My father had sat all night in a hut, holding the edges of the wound together. It healed with a wide scar, nevertheless, and, to cover it, he grew a moustache which he never shaved off. The bull-dog died, years later, after fighting with a badger, and it was my father's pride that the badger, too, was mortally wounded.

My father's eyes, apart from their colour, always seemed remarkable to me. The folds about them were so deep that the eyes seemed almost to be double-lidded, like those of some reptiles and birds. The lashes were sparse and white. They had not become so but had remained like that, for he had been white-headed as a boy and nicknamed 'Snowball'. He had been bandy too, and, although he was so no longer, yet his gait, whether he walked or ran, had something eccentric about it, characteristic of people who have been bow-legged.

Even when very young I was quite familiar with the word 'bandy', and I think there must have been many more people afflicted with bow-leggedness then.

I had ample opportunity to examine my father's face, because he used to take my brother and me, one on each knee, and tell us stories. These kept us quiet and out of the way so that my mother could get on with things that were more important. The stories were, of course, 'a lot of nonsense', and it is only in recent years that I have realised how good the nonsense was, how fluent the inventiveness and how rare the gift. Then, we took it for granted; it was a valueless indulgence like cheap sweets and paper chains at Christmas. The stories were always moral, but not obtrusively so, or we would laugh and refuse to accept anything so obviously designed to 'make us good'. Neither would we accept any stories with characters or a background that were too familiar. It was no use his beginning: 'Once upon a time there was a little boy and a little girl who lived in Arundel Square, North seven.' We wanted fairies, princesses, witches, genii, giants, ogres, goblins, gnomes; primeval forests, deserts, oceans, golden palaces, tents and log huts, pictures in the fire and in the clouds, ivory castles and falling off a rainbow that went out like a light. We had all of these.

In the beginning, I suppose, we were poor, but not very, not so that we suffered any real deprivation. As I first remember, there were only my brother and I, besides my mother and father, and we lived in two rooms on the first floor of a house in Arundel Square. There was the 'front room' which was 'best' and the kitchen where we lived. The front room contained a large double bed, two cots, a piano with its stool, a large sofa with one end that let down, two large armchairs to match, a pedestal table with an oval, polished walnut top and claw legs, an octagonal table with a polished mahogany top, four legs with diagonal stretchers supporting a small tray, four high-backed dining-room chairs, upholstered to match the sofa, an oak wardrobe and a vast mahogany chest of drawers. Over the fireplace was a looking-glass, Gothic in structure, with several small shelves, flanking the central large mirror. In front of this was a great gilt clock on an ebony pediment. Gilt cupids supported the blue enamel face of the clock, which slept under a glass case. On either side of the clock were two candlesticks, also gilded and of the same design. The candlesticks were branched and their glass cases precluded any candles being set into them. There was a pair of flesh-coloured vases, each about two feet in height, with ladies in classical dress painted on them, and a number of pieces

51

of Doulton ware reposed between. Two windows opened on to a balcony overlooking the square. The windows were curtained, first with thick lace and then with red serge and plush. On the floor, in front of each window, stood two ceramic pots the size of small barrels, and these contained the aspidistras. From the walls, with their strongly patterned paper, some sturdily framed etchings looked down on us.

All of these things show that, in the beginning, we were not so very poor.

There was red and green linoleum on the floor and thin, flat, patterned rugs. The room was a jumble of ornaments, chamberpots, toys and pyjamas, Sunday tea, paper bags of sweets and the smell of sunshine on dust. It was our best room all the same.

The kitchen was different and, although we spent most of our lives in it, I do not remember it so well. There was a large sink, in one corner, with a single cold-water tap. Every kind of washing was done at the sink and around it were gathered towels and tea-towels, face-flannels, dish-cloths, medicines and tea-leaves. Under the sink were floor-cloths, rubbish, pipes, disgust and fascination.

The focus of life in the kitchen was the big black range. In winter, the fire was relit by my father every morning. He was an early riser and used to say that bed was a place to die in. If that were so, then it was the one aspect of death that I liked. In winter we always had hot water because kettles rested permanently on top of the stove. There was a big brass fire-guard in front. We had a gas-cooker too, but this was used only when we had no fire. In the centre of the room was a large kitchen table, over the top of which was nailed some 'oil cloth' which I used to pick, so that patches of the thin cotton backing showed through and got covered with grime.

Oddly enough, what I remember most about the table were the sounds of it. My mother used to chop vegetables, holding the point of a knife and moving the handle rapidly up and down. I would dance to this sound, running on tip-toe as fast as I could, till the floor shook, the windows rattled, flakes fell from the ceiling and the lady downstairs came up to complain. The sewing-machine, as it made the table vibrate, was better for dancing, slower and more dignified and, after a while, bright scraps of material and ends of cotton would appear on the floor and I would stop dancing to gather these 'flowers'.

We played another game when the floor was washed. We had to sit with our feet up until parts of the floor were dry. Islands appeared and we could tread on them. They grew, joined and formed continents and soon the whole world was dry again and we could walk everywhere we chose.

In this house, my favourite amenity, and not one often enjoyed, was the verandah. On it my mother grew bulbs in pots. I spent a pleasant half-hour one autumn, taking out these 'onions' and throwing them at people below. It was better still in the following spring and summer when, in spite of this treatment, the hyacinths bloomed and the regal lilies nodded down at the street.

My brother, I think, was a fairly obedient child, not only to my parents but, when he was very young, to me too. Unfortunately nobody would believe that he was able to do half the things I taught him and I was nearly always blamed for having done them myself.

We were not often left alone, except on Monday mornings. The wash-house was far down in the basement. There was a big stone copper with a fire-space tunnelled under it. Occasionally we went down. The fire glowed like a jewel and the copper bubbled, belching scalding steam. My own contribution was to put in a red knitted tie of my brother's and our sheets were pink for months. Water ran down the walls, and the wash-house which smelt of soap, coke and fungi, was full of heat and moisture. Usually we stayed upstairs.

One Monday, while we were thus unsupervised, I became interested in a huge saucepan which I guessed was full of Irish stew. I persuaded my brother to lift it onto the floor. The saucepan was heavy and the gas-stove high, but he managed it quite well. My mother, entering the room to find us standing with pieces of meat and potato clutched in our fists, the jelly oozing through our fingers, refused to believe that it was he who had lifted the saucepan and not I.

An Albino Golliwog*

I was said to have brains and probably more than a pottle, but they were not of a very reliable kind and did not include common sense. As well as these I had large green eyes, a protuberant mouth, full of black teeth, and curly brown hair, this last evidently inherited from my father, since my mother had only what she called 'nine hairs and a bit of cotton'. As for clothes I was not so much dressed as decently covered by garments produced, through what must have been miraculous contrivance, by my mother. But there seemed to be something about me that instantly weakened any elastic that I wore, and my legs, in their spiralling stockings, looked like conch shells. I rarely had a button missing, in the strict sense of the word, since I put them in my pocket, when they came off, but many were retained only by will-power and a single thread. Also I was nearly always very far from where I was meant to be, and when I tried to get from one place to another in less than no time, there followed me, always some inches behind, a bedraggled blue bow,

*The word 'golliwog' was not offensive then as it may be now. The classic golliwogs were of old black woollen stockings, and always home-made so that they seemed to be part of ourselves, our family, and, because of this, they were especially loved. *AR, 1984*

54

invisibly attached by one or two long hairs. It was my familiar, a sleazy, blue butterfly, and, in its way, it symbolised my tenuous hold on reality.

Since I was the eldest, my aquaintance with the streets began fairly late. There were no older children whom my mother would trust to look after me and besides, we were superior to so many of our neighbours. We were snobs in our way. Although we were hungry poor my mother never went out of the house in bedroom slippers or with an apron rolled up under her coat, and my father wore a collar and tie on Sundays, not the spotless white 'choker' which most of the men affected. We were not 'posh' since we never wore anything but clothes that were very plain indeed, or worse, and those who did looked down on us, as we looked down on the aprons and chokers.

Our 'superiority' demanded, also, a way of living that was almost monastic in its strictness. It was slovenly, for instance, to do the week's washing on any day of the week but Monday, snobbish to send it 'out'. It was slovenly to have the midday meal later than one o'clock and snobbish to call it anything but 'dinner'. It was slovenly to run round to local shops on just any day of the week; it was snobbish to buy flowers. My mother's chief characteristic was an unremitting, lifeless energy. She had a thin mouth and tired eyes, like dents in a tin.

Soon after I was first allowed to go out to play alone I wandered down the street and found it deserted by any who were young enough to be of any use. Probably most of the other children were still having their dinners, after I had finished mine. Being superior had its drawbacks. If there had been anyone at all, whether I knew them or not, I would have gone up and offered them a 'go' with my skipping rope or asked for a bite of their apple or a suck of their gob-stopper. This last was an extremely hard, round ball that would fit into one's mouth like an egg into an egg-cup. Each was dyed in layers of very bright colour, purple, nigger pink and poison green. You took the gob-stopper out of your mouth, at intervals, sometimes in order to speak and sometimes to see what colour it had now become. Gob-stoppers were 'common'. I was not allowed to buy one. I was not allowed even to pronounce the word. My only hope was to get a lick of somebody else's.

But there was no one in the street. I kicked around for some time and then it occurred to me to go for a walk. Somebody had told me that if you went first to the right, then to the left and so on, inexorably alternating right and left-hand turnings, you could go quite a long way into strange parts and always be able to find your way back again. I felt that this was a good idea, although I realised that I had not fully grasped the system. What I had grasped was that the system for getting back again would be different, but I did not doubt that I should be able to work it out when I tried. I set off, found a stick and rattled it on other people's railings as I passed. Ralph Roberts's father, who was on night work, came out and shook his fist at me, but he had had to stop to put his trousers on, over his pyjamas, and I was a long way past his house by then.

Now I realise that I can only have turned twice, left along Offord Road, right along Liverpool Road and left again down Park Street, but it seemed a long way and I had crossed Liverpool Road. The pavement in Park Street was broken up by very small cobbled 'roads'. They were probably 'entrances' for commercial vans. This meant that one continually stepped down off the pavement and up again. It made the way seem much longer.

I certainly got somewhere, but grew frightened before my surroundings became strange. I was only in Upper Street, which I knew well, but it was a 'busy' road. I had never been there alone before. People, hurrying by, nearly pushed me over, as I stared vacantly at the traffic, which seemed to be moving in much the same way, and I did not want to be 'jostled' by a tram.

I suddenly felt no more than the six-years-old that I was. I had always been told, 'If ever you are lost, don't go with a stranger; find a policeman.'

He was very tall and it made my arm ache, holding his hand. The people who had brushed past me, before, now began to notice me.

'Poor little thing! She's lost. Poor little thing!'

The policeman must have been going off duty, for we walked, at my pace, to the police station. There I sat on a bench with my feet swinging and policemen, without helmets, came and looked at me. My policeman had very fair hair, almost white. I had decided that I would be afraid of an albino so I asked him if he had pink eyes. He stooped down, smiling, and it was all right. They were blue. Another policeman took me home. In the police station they had given me a bar of chocolate and an apple. The chocolate cost a penny. I kept the wrapper for a long time to show that I too was sometimes able to have this chocolate, thin as a biscuit, very milky and far superior to the sweets we bought for a halfpenny and that were screwed up in squares of newspaper. It was a new experience too, to have a whole apple to myself, since I was always told that I could not eat a whole one and would waste it. It occurred to me, when I had eaten nearly all of this apple, that I might have saved the core just to show what I could do, when given the chance. The stalk was no use for this, so I threw it away. As soon as I was on the doorstep and realised that I had been lost, I burst into tears.

This did not happen the second time. I knew the way to the police station now. Many of the children round our way had been taught to run from the police and never to answer questions. At school they taught that a policeman was a friend and nobody believed it, any more than they spoke at home in the accents recommended by the teachers. We were superior because my parents had the same attitude about police as had the teachers, so I had no hesitation about going to the police station again, and that time I got a custard tart and a fancy cake. They were 'shop-bought' and they were neither broken nor stale. Policemen without helmets came and looked at me again but they were not the same ones. I pouted and sucked in my cheeks. They took me as far as the corner of the street and then I said I was all right and ran on. I was jubilant. I had gone to the police station intending to be 'a poor little thing' and it had worked. It was my first experience of deliberately and successfully 'putting on an act'.

But, the third time, I knew the game was up, as soon as I went in. The fair policeman met me and smiled. He did not say anything but went through a green painted door. After a moment a gust of laughter came out and then another policeman. He told me to go home. I sucked in my cheeks, made my eyes large and stared up at him, but it was no use. I stood on the corner looking at the police station saying to myself that I was lost. I was. After a while I went home.

In Islington, where we lived, anything but wool was discounted as clothing. Nothing else had any warmth in it. All of us children wore many layers and must have looked like teddy-bears or those pin-cushions that are made by winding strips of felt layer upon layer.

Apart from all this there were some cotton garments which were worn not for warmth but as protection against dirt of one kind or another. The material for these came from the meat market, at Smithfield, where one of my uncles was a bummaree. After being discarded by pieces of pork and beef and mutton, it went to clothe us. The meat market material was of two kinds; first there was the ordinary 'meat-cloth', a kind of unbleached knitted stuff which was somewhat elastic. All our face-cloths, dish-cloths and floor-cloths were made of it and, because of its high powers of absorbence, it was of great use on the babies.

The other material was from the packing-cases and was a kind of loosely woven checked gingham, rather of the texture of a fine flour-bag but in various unfortunate colours, so that we were always to be seen in overalls of black and white over-checked with liquorice brown, bilious green, jaundiced yellow or livid mauve.

The things which I shall never forget were the sub-standard stockings. They really were sub-standard. Sometimes they were extremely short and would not keep up, sometimes one was longer than the other, some, which were worse, were of two colours and textures, changing somewhere about the middle of the leg where it could not possibly be made to look like a matter of choice. But the worst, the very dreadful worst, were those with seams up the front.

One day, having just come out of school, I was walking along by the shops with two of my best friends, when I saw my mother coming towards us and carrying a shopping-bag in each hand. My mother was wearing stockings with seams up the front, and the next moment I found myself doing something I had never intended to do; I grabbed my friends, one by each hand, and saying, 'Quick, run!' darted with them through the crowd.

Afterwards I thought I should never get over the shame of it. Nobody at home would speak to me but the cat who was too young to understand. They thought it was because I was too lazy to help to carry home the shopping and I could not explain to anyone that it was because of the stockings with seams up the front, so I sat under the Judas tree in the church gardens and added tears to the other stains that were on Alby.*

*One wet afternoon she decided to make a golliwog. As her mother did not have any suitable black material, she was forced to make it out of white linen sheeting. She was reconciled again to the project by her father's assurance about the existence of Albino Africans with white skin and red hair and her mother's suggestion that she unravel an old red woollen glove to make beautiful curly red hair for 'alby', the much-loved Albino golliwog.

Meals at our house were unusual affairs, for each piece of crockery was unique in its way, the plates and cups and saucers being throw-outs from a pottery. Some was actually thrown out on to a rubbish-dump and we retrieved it, not much chipped. Soon, however, the factory owners got to know that this stuff had a market value. It ceased to appear on the dumps and arrived instead on the market stalls, most of it bearing extraordinary coloured blobs which the unknowing would try to scrape off their plates or fish out of their cups. Sometimes the plates or saucers rocked on the table; sometimes a cup was off balance and, like an old-fashioned tumbler, had to be held upright until it was empty.

We had our useful 'contacts' too, amongst people in the neighbourhood. One of them used to get bread at wholesale prices and sugar a farthing a pound cheaper than retail. The week-end joint came straight from Smithfield. We knew somebody who worked for a builder who was getting rid of some paint that he couldn't sell because it was such an unpopular colour. After that, nearly everything in our house was painted in the same rather disgusting yellow, mustard laced with Worcester sauce. At one time, our father worked in a soap factory. Nobody would have thought that anyone working in such a clean-sounding job could have smelt as peculiar as he did. He, too, could get a commodity at wholesale prices, but perhaps we did not value it sufficiently to be willing to pay for it. Instead, we used an extraordinary waste product which was brought home like pease pudding in sheets of newspaper. It was whitish green, soft and sticky and, kept in jars or saucers by the kitchen sink, was used almost exclusively. With hot water, it produced a stiff glutinous lather which it was impossible to rinse off entirely; in cold water it merely slithered over one's skin. But at least we had made a gesture towards cleanliness and we felt we were not quite beyond the pale.

High, black, spiked railings surrounded Arundel Square and lindens with sooty boles and a sticky excrescence from their leaves stood there, as though they had been waiting for years to get out. Groups of disconsolate privet waited too, round the feet of the lindens, like children, with black-trousered adults, in a funeral group. When it rained the pavement under the trees was slippery with black slime and always the place smelt of cats. I had not then become aware of the scent of linden blossom. Perhaps these lindens never flowered. The only good smell about the square was the autumn one of heaped leaves smouldering.

Within the railings were no flowers, but gravel paths, rank grass and two tennis-courts. On one side of the square were the allotments and the railway. Even after we moved to Ellington Street, I used to go back to the square to play. We had no key to it by then, but I was used to 'climbing over'.

Once in my life I made what I felt to be a large contribution to the food of the family, but it cost me dear. I had always thought that if ever I climbed the railings by the railway I should instantly be run over by a train and I was about eight before I managed to do it. Once over, I noticed some strange plants. I had never seen anything like them before. I pulled one up and found a carrot on the end of it. I started to pull them up as fast as I could, using both hands. I got onions, turnips, beetroots, potatoes and a cabbage. I had no pockets, but I wore some voluminous bloomers. They had been cut down for me and I hated them. I prayed that the elastic would hold and stuffed all the vegetables into these. Running frantically through the streets on skinny little legs and desperately clutching my sagging, bulging stomach, I must have looked like a little alley cat about to have kittens.

When I got home I hid all the vegetables in the scullery. They were not found until I was in bed. My parents were not in favour of stealing, but I did not get into trouble. My father found me in tears and thought that anyone as remorseful as that had been punished enough. I had, but it wasn't remorse. It was only that, when I undressed, I found a large green caterpillar crawling on my skin.

As for other things necessary to near normal, civilised existence, it was 'just a question of knowing'. There was a 'cut-price' shop at the other end of the main street, and there you could save as much as a shilling on the week's shopping by paying careful attention to prices. And there was the Caledonian Market on Tuesdays and Fridays. This was a cattle market on other days of the week and the cattle-pens made intriguing gymnastic apparatus during school holidays.

Our treats were inexpensive too, for, mostly, we went on picnicking expeditions, perhaps very seldom, but they live, in memory, as days which changed the whole of our lives and all our summers were coloured by them. We took thick sandwiches, sour apples, carefully halved, and bottles of water.

There were some woods and, surely, they were at Highgate? I now know people who live at Highgate and I cannot think that the woods were then so near. The ground was soft and leaf-mouldy and I was constantly disappointed because there were no bluebells. There never could be any bluebells, for, whenever we went, the trees had been long in leaf and it was much too late in the year, but how could we know this, we who, moved by the desire to perpetuate ourselves, stole wet cement which we pressed on to a wall to cut our names in.

But, at Totteridge, there were buttercups, an abundance, a wealth, a waste of buttercups, like gold lifted clear of the ground in an outpouring of joy. When it really came to it, in spite of our constant preoccupation with tales of exploration and high adventure, we never went farther than two open fields away. How could we? There were more flowers than we could pick in just one, and we spent all day gathering and gathering. It was like trying to clear the seashore of sand. There was so much and we would not be able to come again for such a long time. It was pain to look back at that vast abandonment of wealth which ordinary, childish, physical limitations forbade our taking away.

Sometimes we went fishing. We had relatives who lived near the Wanstead Flats. My mother said that this was almost 'East End' and not superior. These relatives belonged to the darker side of the family and I do not know how they were connected. They wore chokers and bedroom slippers. They were always extremely kind to us children and my mother was always extremely aloof towards them. Each year they would bring us a piece of Christmas pudding and we gave them a piece of ours. Their pudding was the colour of brown paper and tasted faintly bitter, as though there were carbolic in it.

Every time you ate a piece of somebody else's Christmas pudding it was the guarantee of one happy month in the coming year. To refuse it was as unlucky as wiping off a kiss. My mother used to shudder as she swallowed the smallest piece possible.

All their food tasted horrible, but we were always too hungry to mind very much, and in our own street lives we often consumed worse. (We picked and ate the soft leaves of linden trees and stole lumps of pitch to put in our mouths. This was as good as chewing gum, once it softened, although it tasted oddly.) My mother told us that we 'didn't want to go there', but we did, and when they came to see us and invited us to their house, at some unspecified time, I learned, as I got older, to insist on fixing the date so that we really did go. This occurred at most twice a year, but the pleasure from it ran through all the summer.

The flats were probably just a fetid marsh. To us they were a lake. This lake was so shallow that nowhere did the water come higher than one's thighs (except accidentally), and the lake was so vast that it was possible to stand in it and see around only a sheet of water and a thin line of moth-eaten grass in the distance. Children stood in couples dotted all about, like birds, and the mud was ankle deep.

Frightened sticklebacks buried themselves in the mud and their spines stuck into bare feet. Every so often a child would raise one foot, pick off a tiddler and pop it into the jar which hung round his neck. The real fishing was done with an onion sack; two people held the ends and, stooping, walked along with it taut between them in the water. Together they lifted the sack; the sticklebacks escaped with the water and the mud, leaving the angrily whiskered gudgeon jumping about like cats on hot bricks. We caught snails and a huge fresh-water mussel.

The blessed peace did not last long, for my brother and I often quarrelled and there came the inevitable moment when neither would carry back the sack alone. We each held a corner and stared obstinately at one another. Little waves slapped our rolled-up clothes with gentle malice.

'If you let go', said my brother, 'so shall I.'

Then, as if in answer to a prayer, there floated towards us, out of the reeds, a shallow box. It bobbed there with sinister suggestiveness.

'We could float it back in the box,' said my brother.

We picked up the sack and twisted out most of the water. I put Alby in the box first to give him a ride. Then we put the folded sack on top of him and the whole lot sank.

I hesitated not at all before I held my nose, shut my eyes, and plunged. For a moment, the only part of me that was above the surface was the part that was already wet from the malicious little waves. Alby was sorrier than ever when I brought him up and I was a sorry sight myself. My brother had a way of laughing very deeply and quite silently. His face screwed up so that only the tears that squeezed themselves out, as though from slits in a lemon, showed where his eyes were. He shook so rapidly that he seemed to be still. My brother laughed in the way that a top spins.

'Never mind!' he said at last, in a tiny pip of a voice that seemed to be shaken out of him. 'You'll dry in the sun.'

He was in a good mood since I had managed to rescue the sack which was precious, for it was difficult to persuade a greengrocer to give you one when all you ever bought from him was a few pennyworths' of pot-herbs and some potatoes; also he had been 'good', while I should obviously be in big trouble when I got home. However well I dried out, I could not disguise what had happened to me, and Alby looked even worse than before, the parts of him that had been white being now a dismal khaki. The mud was so sticky and opaque that, when we came out of the water, we were wearing socks of it. While we were unsuccessfully trying to remove this, I noticed something which made me think that I was dreaming.

Near the bank were a few stunted water-lily leaves and, seated on one of them, a frog no larger than a little finger-nail. It was the sort of thing one read about but never saw, like bluebells, the sort of thing one only half believed in, like elves and squirrels and wild rabbits and God. These things belonged to books, not to real life. But then, looking minutely into the grass about us we saw dozens – hundreds of these little brown frogs, swarming, like cockroaches.

For a moment we played with the idea of emptying the jar of fish and taking home the frogs instead. We would never find another jar, for these, returned to the grocer, were worth a halfpenny each. At last we found a cardboard cigarette box and filled it with wet weed and tiny frogs.

Being wet seemed to have made me tired, and I sat in the bus half asleep and looking at the pattern on the upholstered seats and then at the slatted floor. I noticed something like a large insect crawling along and thought how strange it was to see a spider in a bus. I wondered why one never did. There were no cobwebs either. While I was looking dreamily at this spider, it suddenly hopped. It was a frog.

The box in my brother's pocket was open and all the frogs were coming out. There they were, when one looked closely, on the seats, on the floor, on people! We tried to gather them up, unobtrusively, but the thin lady behind us began to make a fuss and the conductor came to see. He turned us off the bus and what happend to the frogs that were left behind we never knew.

No Grass in our Garden

I learnt to run before I could walk, but I do not remember it. The technique was similar to that employed by an athletic sprinter: he crouches on all fours, knees half bent and stern in air, the weight of his body, which is thus thrown forward, being taken partly by the tips of his fingers resting on the ground. At the crack of the pistol he draws back his hands, while maintaining his stance, and has to keep running so as not to fall over. At eleven months my mastery of this was imperfecct and the experiment ended with my splitting my head on the fender. All the same, as a means of locomotion the technique is not a bad one and I seem to have used a modified form of it for a good many years.

Our house was at the Westbourne Road end of

Ellington Street which sloped down towards Liverpool Road. It dipped steeply towards the bottom and the pavement was cracked and uneven where the dip occurred. This part of the street and the lamp-post near it were the scene of most of my minor accidents. It was here that I received nearly all of my visible scars.

Our house boasted a front 'garden', and giving entrance to it was a gate which was usually jammed shut. There was a kind of flattened horseshoe instead of a latch. It was rusty and squeaked as the gate was opened or closed. The front garden was quite full of knot grass and this I accepted, for it seemed to me to be a fairly attractive substitute for a lawn and better than mud or dust. It looked down on to an 'area' which we called an 'airy' and which was protected by a kind of roof of iron railing on which I used to walk, until I slipped once.

It must have been a wonderfully hot, sunny summer's day for, afterwards, I lay, bruised, grazed, oiled and bandaged in the knot grass amidst the smell of petrol fumes, horse dung and tarry dust from the roads. It was only on very hot days that we were ever allowed to do this because of the cold and the damp that would 'strike up' from the ground.

The back garden was less pleasant, bare as the asphalt playground at school, but more treacherous, in that it was uneven, packed hard with pebbles in clay. The back of the house was to the north, so that this garden rarely got any sun and was, in any case, not so much shaded as darkened by three of the ubiquitous, sooty, sticky lindens, which rose as tall as the three-storeyed houses at the end of the garden, against the smoke-grimed, crumbling brick wall.

My mother liked the trees because they prevented our being 'overlooked' in summer by the inhabitants of Bride Street (how inaptly named!). I did not. I wanted a garden, but, wherever one dug, one came on the spreading roots of the trees, sapping the life out of the ground. The trees seemed to me to be a respectable green screen around the sordid isolation of the garden, themselves precluding any graciousness and beauty that we could be proud to show. I hated these trees and, when I remembered, futilely cut and sawed at the roots.

I wanted a lawn and this seemed possible, for surely a lawn was just grass. So I began to take the garden in hand. Every time I went out I dug up a tuft of grass from somewhere and carried it home, roots and earth and all. This I pressed on to the stony ground and watered. Once I succeeded in making a patch of green about the size of the seat of a kitchen chair. But, either through cats or the sun and the wind, always the lawn ended in the same way, as a few dry scattered tufts, looking like nothing so much as the lumps of matted hair that are dragged from a slut's comb. Grass grew everywhere, even between paving-stones, but it would not grow in our garden.

Then, one autumn, for a few months, my father worked in the gardening department of a large London store and brought home dozens, countless dozens of jonquil bulbs. There was one thing for which my mother would never forgive my father. I overheard her say so. Perhaps it was the bulbs, for, if he bought them, they must have cost quite all of a week's wage. We planted them around the edge of the garden against the dingy walls.

And they came up. April was full of flowers that year and, above, the lime trees made a delicate rough-cut net that was sewn with leaf buds.

Then, when all the border was quick with jonquils, calculating creatures that we were, we began to count them, so that we could boast of how many we had. There were hundreds, and every day new flowers opened as the early sun shone from the Liverpool Road, along the deep trough, between the houses, to where our garden lay, and we counted again in the late April evenings when the sun had forgotten to go down.

Soon the blooms began to die, we picked them off, the number dwindled and we did not count any more. Something must have happened to them after that, for they did not come up another year and the garden returned to nearly its old form. Only two things were added and those by me; they were a little rockery, under the trees in each of the far corners of the garden. I piled earth there and then managed to procure a number of 'rocks' which I pressed into it. They were not really rocks but lumps of concrete with stones embedded. I cannot remember how or when I got them, but they were the kind of thing one sees lying around where roads are being drilled. They must have been heavy and I could not have been very big, for these events all occurred before I was eleven and became too refined for such efforts. The rockeries were useful when we wanted to climb over the wall. Not a leaf ever grew on them.

Steps led up to our front door which was varnished and artificially 'grained'. By hanging precariously over the area, one could climb from the railings of the top step on to the window-sill of our front room. It was usually possible to prise up the window.

The bedroom occupied by my parents was on the same floor, separated from the front room by large communicating doors which were never opened.

The passage was ours and stairs went up from it to where other people lived. Four stairs went down from it to our own wonderfully large lavatory. At street level, this was the only part of our accommodation that stimulated our imagination. The lavatory had a small window, about eighteen inches square, small enough to be worth aiming at with a ball from the garden, small enough to be excitingly difficult to climb through when we let ourselves down into the garden on a 'rope' made from bed-clothes knotted together. We could not do this from any other window, first because the only window at this level and at the back of the house was that of my parents' bedroom. It was only about a six-foot drop from this to the roof of the coal-shed and that was no use, besides, in the lavatory, we could lock ourselves in and thus escape discovery. Once my brother was commanded to come out, but he pushed the bed-clothes through the window to me, in the garden, before he did so.

This ruse was not as successful as it might have been, because we could not help going into fits of laughter over it. We were punished for being 'up to something', but our mother never did discover just what it was we were 'up to'.

We always planned to get out of my parents' bedroom window if ever there were a fire in the night. I cannot think why, because we slept downstairs at the back, at garden level, and if we had been in either of the two rooms on the ground floor, we could have walked out of the front door.

The coal-shed was divided into three, but we did not use our part for coal because, being in the basement, we had a cellar. My brother and I used to play in the shed. For a while it was a zoo and we kept in it all the spiders and caterpillars, tadpoles and fishes that we collected during the summer. We had no idea how to take care of these creatures, and they did not live very long.

For most of the time the shed was a 'house'. The floor of it was only about a yard square and we found a piece of old coconut matting to put down. Then we brought in all the toy animals and dolls and found boxes for ourselves. After this we did nothing but sit on the boxes, enjoying the closed-in atmosphere of the 'house'.

The shed soon began to smell strongly of mildew. Our mother said that the mat was probably rotting and we must take it out and air it. Unfortunately we had put it directly on to the earth floor and it was now in a state of disintegration, but worse than this, under the matting was a very large earthworm.

I do not usually mind worms, nor caterpillars, nor

slugs, nor harmless snakes, nor anything that crawls. I was not afraid to touch bits of fluff as my brother was, and I was not much afraid of the dark, at least, rarely so much afraid that the fear became uncontrollable and I could not walk into darkness when necessary. But the sight of this particular worm, in the enclosed and secret atmosphere of the little house, gave me a shock of hysterical fear and loathing. I could not touch it and I could not let it remain. I went into the scullery, got a bottle of ammonia and tipped it on to the earthworm. I do not know what prompted me to do this, unless my mother had given me an exaggerated idea of the corrosive powers of ammonia, because she did not want me to touch it. I thought that death would be instantaneous and it was not. The memory of this incident tortured me for many nights. It sickens me still.

Being superior we were allowed out less than most, but my happiest memories are of playing in the street and of our street companions. One of the pleasantest of these lived at the back of us, in Bride Street, and his name was 'Jackie'.

We were a cut above Bride Street and certainly the houses did look dirtier and poorer than those in Ellington Street. The only reason we were ever allowed to go into Bride Street was that there was a little group of shops there, including a sweetshop, a public house and a fish and chip shop. We never had fish and chips. It was probably too expensive.

On summer Sunday mornings, when the windows were open, there was always the sound of raucous singing and a clatter of cans and crockery from Bride Street and there was the sound of hens clucking and the crowing of a cock in someone's garden. Why the cock should have crowed only on Sunday is a mystery, since Friday seems more appropriate, but certainly these sounds are associated only with Sunday.

Jackie was younger than either of us and lived at the

71

top of the house that backed on to ours. He used to look out of the window and call down to us, and, one day, he threw down one end of a long clothes-line. We tied a 'message' on the end and he pulled it up again. This method of communication was difficult, because of the trees, and eventually he was allowed to come out to play with us.

Like most children round our way, we had a soap-box on wheels, which we called a 'trolley'. Even in this we were superior, for ours had been painted with the unattractive paint that my father had got for nothing. Jackie's mother liked him in pink and it did suit him. He had black bobbed hair cut with a fringe on his forehead, black, mischievous eyes, a round rosy face and a beautiful laughing red mouth out of which he spoke with a cockney accent so pronounced that even we, sometimes, could not understand him. He wore polished black shoes, little white socks and very short, pale pink trousers with a little belted pink tunic over them. By the time we sent him home everything about him was grey, and it was not long before he came out in some dark garments that had been roughly made out of some old ones of his father's. He was proud of these and we regarded them with approval.

All three of us would pile on to our trolley and go tearing down the hill. Nearly always Jackie was in tears, at least once, for he sat in front to steer and got the brunt of it when we hit the lamp-post or shot into the gutter. Always he laughed as the tears made tracks on his rosy cheeks. His nose ran and he never had a handkerchief. He liked playing with us.

One day a gipsy came to our door and I answered it. She was a very dark and frightening gipsy and wore gold ear-rings and a man's felt hat. We always said 'No, thank you' to hawkers and they usually went away.

The gipsy was angry and insulting and I did not know the meaning of half the words she said, but I understood her last taunt, which she spoke with malicious gentleness, as she went down the steps: 'Is father out of work, dear, that you can't afford it?'

Trembling, I asked her politely to shut the gate in order to keep the dogs out. She left it wide open and I was far too frightened to go down and shut it myself.

As I went back downstairs into the kitchen I knew that the gipsy had been right and wondered at her powers of divination. I had not known before, but I knew now; our father was one of the unemployed.

And many things which I had noticed out of the tail of my mind I now faced squarely; that my father always had time to walk half-way to school with me, that he would not tell me where he worked and that whenever he came home in the evening my mother said: 'Any good?' as he entered the door, and he always shook his head. But he was never there when I came home to dinner. Where did they go, all these unemployed men, and what did they do all day, wandering about away from the house, so that the children should remain unaware of the family's plight? And mostly they had not even the price of a cup of tea in their pockets. The worst part of unemployment was the shame of it.

At school there were four of us who, by reason of our intelligence, were considered likely winners of scholarships, at eleven. For this reason we missed certain classes so that we should, as quickly as possible, reach a class where scholarship work was taught and we could spend one or two years at it. The names of the others were Titchy Gammon, Violet Leicester and Harry Gomm. We four became friends simply because, through our rapid promotion, we lost touch with other people of our age. Titch and I were the closest friends. Harry, being a boy, played in the other playground and Violet was odd. She was the gentlest creature I have ever met. She crept about like a bee that is woken in winter, and her hands and her voice were so soft as to be almost ineffectual.

73

Even her legs were smooth, not mottled and sand-blasted like ours. Her hair was black and her face like parchment, with tiny threads of blood beneath the skin.

Harry was a fair, fresh-complexioned, matter-of-fact child, with an air of considering carefully everything he said. It was Harry who asked one of the teachers where babies came from. We all grinned and she smiled self-consciously and told him to ask his mother. He said he had done so, but she would not tell him. We all 'knew', of course, but Harry was not the kind of person to be satisfied with any unsubstantiated rumour. Presumably he did eventually find someone to give him more information for it was he who told us about sexual intercourse. We were standing in Westbourne Road at the time. Violet said she did not believe it and closed her pale lips firmly. After a while she mentioned a bishop who had come to talk to us at Sunday school. We all remembered him.

Violet whispered: 'He's got a daughter, hasn't he? Well, do you mean to say that he did?'

Harry hesitated, obviously shaken in his conviction. But I knew that he had been right. It fitted so perfectly with adult jokes that I had overheard and with my own vague sensations. I felt that this would be the logical culmination of them. Besides, I did not have Violet's faith in the behaviour of adults. But when I tried to argue, I found that I had no words in which to say what I meant. And, suddenly, Titch turned on Harry, her eyes bright with tears and her tiny figure trembling. She slapped his face, so that he staggered, and then ran away. She sped towards Sonning Street, where she lived, running with quick, nervous movements of her match-stick arms and legs and jerkily, like the motion pictures we infrequently saw. At any other time we would have run after Titch and started a fight, yet, now, we knew that, for some reason, she was beside herself and, by tacit consent, neither Harry nor I did anything about it. Dear

Harry, with his honesty and his innocence, was up against more than he knew.

For some time I had known, also, about menstruation, but discussed this only with older girls. I was very tall and, at school, in a high class for my age. I think that many of my acquaintances did not realise that I was only nine years old. By the time I was nearly eleven some of the girls I knew had turned fourteen and had left school. I still met them in the street in the evenings. They carried handbags and wore light stockings and high-heeled shoes. Their skirts were short, nearly up to their knees and, most exciting of all, they wore long silk knickers and fancy garters. (These are an aspect of the fashions of the twenties to which the recent revival has failed to do justice.) Sometimes my brother and I would imitate these girls who, when they ran, wrapped their skirts round them, tightly, clamped their knees together and kicked their heels sideways, but, in some ways, I wanted to be like them.

I was often in fights, but only one is memorable, and that is the one I had with Flossy Bray. She lived along our street and her father was a bus-conductor. The first thing I remember about her is that she was absent from school when I was promoted to the class in which we became acquainted. She had had scarlet fever and, when she came back, everyone crowded round her. My mother said I should keep away because I might still catch it. In spite of this she and I became sufficiently friendly for me to lie about my age, so that I should be put in her class at Sunday school. She had an umbrella and we used to drop our 'collection' halfpennies into it, so that we could buy sweets with them later.

She was ten and I was only eight. I still say she started it, by pushing me against a lamp-post which had just been painted a vivid moss green. The lamp-post was not merely sticky, it was quite wet and the palms of my hand were as green as though they belonged to a giant frog, after I had grasped it to prevent myself falling into the gutter. Flossy laughed, but came too near, so that I pushed one hand into her face. Then she wiped her own hands round the lamp-post and slapped me. We began slapping each other as fast as we could, getting fresh supplies of paint at intervals. We moved down the street. There were more lamp-posts and more paint. Soon the lower parts of most of the lamp-posts were almost denuded. Flossie looked spectral and macabre and there was paint on her brand-new panama hat. I found a handkerchief and wiped my face, which probably smeared it a little. Then Flossie and I went home, separately.

The looks of people I met should have told me that I would not get away with it, although I tried to walk into the house as though nothing had happened, except that I was a little late.

While my father was cleaning me with turpentine, my mother wrote a note to Flossie's mother to say that Flossie and I were not to play together any more. As I ran down the street to put the note in their letter-box I passed a turpentine-washed Flossie, running up it, to put a note in ours. I had the advantage and beat her by two houses and the top step, but I suppose they won, since Flossie's mother had written her note in the third person.

At school our form was divided into those who were 'grown up' and those who were not. It was a matter of great interest and a constant topic of conversation. We exaggerated it all shamelessly and pretended to be in pain whether we were or not. Almost the only people who were practical and helpfully informative about it were the Jewesses. Stoke Newington was not far away and many Jewish people were in business there and sent their daughters to our school. I was but vaguely aware that their outlook was different from ours and better in its frank acceptance. Only much later did I come to

76

realise how much I was affected by contact with these girls and the women of their families.

At home we had no bathroom. Baths were occasionally taken in a large zinc vessel that was set on pads of newspapers in front of the kitchen fire, but, as we grew older, this became more and more difficult, for the kitchen was our living-room too.

I was just prepared for a bath when I realised that I was menstruating. This had not happened to me before and I did not know what to do. At school there were many taboos concerning monthly periods; one must not go swimming, eat ice-cream, wash in cold water, do gym, nor have a bath. But I had never discussed it with my mother and the shock was too great for me to want to do so now. Besides, half the family had been sent out of the house and my mother was upstairs with the twins. Trembling, I had my bath as quickly as possible. I was almost certain that I should die. Everyone else in my form at school, next day, was almost certain too. I sat in my desk, doubled up, with my hands across my stomach, as everybody else did at such times. My friends looked at me with sympathy. Several of them asked me if I felt all right. Unfortunately for the drama of the situation, I did.

About four weeks later I began to feel worried because it did not happen again. I knew all about it, of course, although I was not sure whether the months should be lunar or calendar. I thought that I had harmed myself for life and was sure that the final consequences would be terrible. I must be grown up; I had to bring it on somehow. I jumped down the basement stairs and then broke some of the springs of the prickly green sofa by turning somersaults on it. After this the room began to reel. It was, of course, the old equilibrium trouble, but I did not connect it and thought that the dizziness was a symptom of the dire disease I had caused in myself.

I did have another period but, by then, nobody at school found it so interesting because, most inappropriately, nothing awful had happened to me. Only Sonia was troubled because, she said, I must tell my mother and I could not see that this was necessary. The holidays began and still I had not told her. Sonia wrote me an urgent, anxious letter which I read and put away at the bottom of my sewing-box. My mother took out the letter and read it. She always did this, but I had not yet had enough letters of my own to realise that she did it. She told me that she had found my letter by accident, and asked what it was that Sonia wanted me to tell her. It took nearly a whole day to get it out of me. Then she said: 'Is it that you've started or just that you know about it?' I said I had known about it since I was eight, and it struck me suddenly that she knew nothing at all of our school life, our conversations and our interests. She said that, during a period, I must not eat ice-cream, go swimming, wash in cold water, and have a bath, and any respect that I had had for her vanished as did my confidence in her. I resolved then that for my sisters it should be different.

The Scarlet Thread
as told to Rachel Barton

About the author and the book

Sita Devi was born in 1958 in a small village in Northern India, the youngest daughter of a large family. She remembers the countryside there with affection, describing the rose-filled hedgerows, the tall old trees and fields of wheat, maize and sugar cane. She remembers too her village of narrow, shady streets and the houses of red clay and brick where they could sleep on the flat roof in the hot season, watching the moon and stars.

Sita's family were poor and her parents had to work hard to support them. Her mother often left home at 4 a.m. for her work as a seamstress, struggling to earn enough to see that all her children – two sons and five daughters – had a good education.

Sita knew that one day her parents would choose a husband for her, and she trusted them to make a wise choice. However, things did not turn out as she had anticipated.

My name is Sita Devi. I was born in a small village in north-west India twenty-eight years ago. Now I am a British citizen and I have lived in the UK for nearly thirteen years. I know something of how people here live; I have visited their homes, seen their family life, heard about their work and joined them in their leisure; I even know something about the way they think. But the people here know nothing of how we live at home in India, or even how we live over here so close to them.

Sometimes they think they know better than I do. A school teacher I spoke to once said, 'It must be terrible for you in India to see so many people ill and starving around you.' I said, 'But I have not seen this; everyone in our village had enough to eat, even the poorest, and most were quite healthy.' He became angry and started to shout at me. 'You are so ignorant, you must know that Indian people are starving.'

I can only tell of what I have seen, or know for certain, and I will write everything as truly as I can. I do not think that any Indian woman has done this before, certainly not an uneducated girl like me. Perhaps there are some things I have not understood correctly, or have not paid enough attention to. It is only in the last year or so that I have started to think about my life. Now my English friend is writing down for me what I tell her.

Most people here seem to think we live in shacks in India, all crowded together, with everything dirty and wretched about us. It may be so for some in the big cities, but I will tell you how we lived in our village of about one thousand people.

All around us are the plains, stretching far far away, where many crops are grown – wheat and maize, sugar cane, vegetables, and the yellow-flowered mustard. Roses grow on the hedges between the fields. Our village is beautiful, quite like an English village. There are many trees in the squares and beside the houses. Many people have a little land and grow flowers and vegetables. The

81

trees give welcome shade and are useful for tethering animals. Our tree is very tall and very old, it is called a 'Nime'. There are many canals in our part of the country, some of them like big rivers with smaller branches bringing water to every part of the land. One such canal flows near our village. The water is clean and clear and we can see little fishes in it. There is also a lake, and here the farmers take their buffaloes and oxen and other animals to drink. Roads leading to and from the village are lined with fine shady trees, some of which have flowers and fruit in season, like the chatoot and behr, and we can pick them as we go along. As children we loved to do this.

The village streets are rather narrow, but this makes them shady in hot weather. Some houses, their outer walls smooth and red, are made of clay which we fetch from the edge of the lake. Others are more modern and made of cement, brick or concrete. Our house is partly clay and part brick. It belongs to my father, who had it from his father. Now my second brother lives there with his family. The roof is flat and we can sit there in the day and sleep there in the hot season as most people do. It is lovely to lie under the still sky and watch the moon and the stars, very big and bright. We have very light beds made of a wooden frame covered with woven material, and these can be easily taken up to the roof and down again. This is useful if it suddenly starts to rain in the night and we have to hurry to shelter. If it turns cold we do not worry as we have quilts to cover us. The women and children sleep in one part and the men in another, or on the verandahs. The older women would often tell stories to us children, or read from a book. We had electricity in our house, and could bring a wire up from downstairs if we wished. Other times we would all sing togther.

There is a courtyard in front of our house and a big room on the ground floor. We did not live in this room but every day one of my elder sisters would wash it over in preparation for the neighbours to come. Five or six women from our street would come every forenoon to sit with us, bringing their food and their work. We all sat on woven rugs on the floor. They made baskets and mats and bedcovers, did embroidery or made up saris. Others would bring baskets of grain and pick out the stones and grit before it was ground. These things they made were for their homes or, if unmarried, for their dowries. There would be much gossiping, laughing, singing, or some-times quarrelling. I sat and listened to them, but as the youngest I did not work. I enjoyed the company and all the interest of their talk, and learned much about the village. It was impossible to be bored or lonely in our house. When the time for the evening meal drew near all the women went away to prepare for the men coming home from work.

Behind the big room there are two smaller rooms. One of these is used by the women as a bathroom and is also a grain store. My mother had made this store herself out of cement, and it is like a big deep box, always filled with wheat or maize. She did not buy the grain but earned it by her work as a seamstress. We had so much we could always sell some of it. In this room were two big iron buckets that were filled with water from a hand pump just outside. This was spring water, also used for cooking. Every day we poured the water from the buckets over ourselves or, when we were young, our mother would do it for us. This is the normal custom in the village. Mother used to get up at four o'clock in the morning, and even if it was cold, pour water over herself from the pump to wake herself up; she had to work so hard. Then she would often make our dinner before she went to work. The men washed in a little shed beside the house near the hand pump. On our small piece of land we also had a garden where Mother grew vegetables and flowers, and there was a shed for the animals. Most villagers keep a cow and a buffalo if they can afford it. Buffalo milk is very rich. We made our own butter, using a small hand churn, and had the buttermilk to drink. We also made our own cheese, but we did not have a buffalo after we became poorer. Some people keep goats too. All these animals are sometimes kept in the ground-floor room, but we never did this.

Every day my brother would go on his bike to the farmer to buy grass for the animals, bringing it back in a big cloth, as we had no grazing. This was not enough for them so we gave them household scraps and fodder bought from the store. Every day, too, they must be taken to the canal to drink and refresh themselves. Otherwise they were just tethered. One bad thing about the village was the flies, and that was the same, I think, everywhere in India. Having the animals so near attracts them, and although we had sprays to kill them they always seemed just as numerous. Mosquitoes too are horrible, especially in those days when few families had nets, and at night our happy sleep was often disturbed by them.

Upstairs was our living room and bedrooms. Although we usually sit on the floor on mats, we had chairs here, and a settee made by hand out of wood. There was also a big wooden bed where sometimes my father or brother slept. Married people do not sleep in the same bed, or even in the same room, unless they are newly weds. This is very different from the custom over here. In fact, we all sleep in various places as we can so easily put our mats and quilts down on the floor, which is always kept very clean. There were nine people in my family so we had several cupboards for our clothes, and ropes slung across the corners where more things could be hung. Our meals were often cooked outside in the courtyard in an earthenware stove that could be carried about. It was filled with wood or coal or dried cow dung, which we would light and wait until it was really hot, then we could cook on top. It may seem odd to use cow dung, but it is good fuel. It is made into round 'cakes' when still wet, and then thrown against the side of the house to dry. We had several other stoves – one was for paraffin – so we could cook many dishes at once.

While in Britain people tend to live behind closed doors; ours in the village are always open. It is never really cold, even in winter, and we can live very much outside. We also like to do things together and we do not lead private lives in the village. For instance, morning and evening when we used to go to the toilet, the women would go in one direction and the men in another, just to the fields. We would squat down among the grass and bushes and make it quite a social occasion. Hindus are bodily very clean; we wash all over each day and wash our hands before meals. We must wash our private parts after going to the toilet, so we usually take water with us. Some villagers had cesspits near their houses, a few had flush toilets, but they did not always use them. One year a village man who had worked in England wrote and told his family that he was returning with his bride, a wealthy English girl. The parents improved their house and even bought and installed a flush toilet for her use. She was very friendly and stayed a long time, but when she left the toilet was not used as it was too good to use.

*

I have never been able to return to my village so I do not know how it is now, but many Indians do go home and they tell me about the changes there. It is remarkable, but there is hardly a family without some member in the UK. Most of them work hard and make money, and much of it is sent back home to their own families. Because of this, and because there is now gas and electricity for all, there is more convenience than before. Many have built fine new houses, just as good as the ones we see in the suburbs over here, and inside there are TV sets, gas stoves, washing machines and refrigerators, as well as modern furniture and ornaments. I have noticed that there are good things and bad things in my part of India, and different good things and bad things here. This is rather confusing. When some things that are good here are taken to the Indian village, like washing machines, it improves life in some ways but spoils it in others. For instance, when I was a child the women would carry their big wash to the lake together, taking the children and food for a picnic. Sitting at the edge of the water with their soap and washboards they would rub the clothes clean as they talked and sang and argued as usual. The children would run around and play together, and when it was time to eat, fires would be lit, tea made, and chapatis cooked with other delicious things to eat. No one was in a hurry and the summer days were long. All these things the women did together made them close, and usually they would help each other in time of need.

There were grocery shops in the village, but no others. To buy other things we had to go to the nearest town or wait for a fair to pass by. Since shop goods were dear and not as well made as those made at home, most village people seldom bought them. So the women and girls were always busy making things in ways they had learned from their mothers and grandmothers. My sisters were also very clever in this way and could make quilts and pillowcases, saris and blouses, and decorate them with embroidery. These things were often beautiful, and very skilfully made; the women enjoyed making them and were proud of their good work. Now people in the village have more money and travel more to the towns. They can get cheap goods there and it does not seem worthwhile to make their own.

Oxen were always used to draw the plough, pull carts and so on, but now I hear that tractors and other kinds of machinery are used by many farmers. This is another reason why the village is better off. Perhaps the farm animals will go in time, but I hope I will be able to go back home before everything is changed too much. Some improvements I will enjoy if I do go; for instance, a new ice factory and the many new shops in the village.

Most Indian women love dress; it is a very important part of our lives. I have always done so, even as a small girl. Because my mother worked as a seamstress she had many pieces of material kept in a big chest. I loved to see all the different colours and feel the textures of the cloth, and I was always begging for new dresses or tunics and trousers. Little girls in the village could wear bright and pretty clothes until they started their periods. After that they should dress very quietly and wear their hair simply braided in one plait. Girls looked forward to marriage because then they could wear beautiful saris, denied to unmarried girls, use make-up, and wear jewellery of gold and silver. Although we were quite poor I always had lovely clothes because of my mother, but I never felt I had enough. I wanted to dress like the wealthier girls in the village, so sometimes I would steal some pretty pieces from my mother's chest and persuade a neighbour to make me a dress. Then mother would be angry because she was keeping the materials for our dowries.

When I was about five years old I longed to wear earrings, so I took a long sharp thorn and pushed the point into my ear lobe. It hurt me and the end broke off and stayed in my ear. I never told anyone and it is still there! Soon after I heard that a neighbour was piercing ears with a needle and thread, so I went along and asked her to do mine. Two friends held me still while she pushed the needle through, but it was very painful and I screamed and struggled as she did the other ear. Afterwards I was glad. She left a piece of thread in each hole to keep it open, but now I know that she should have sterilised the needle, as my ears became infected and for some time I had sores on both sides. It was about three months before they cleared up, and when I put my earrings in the infection started again because they were made of cheap metal, not silver, gold or steel. That did not stop me loving to wear earrings, as I still do.

One day my vanity led me into more trouble. Like most Indian girls I had long thick black hair which I wore in a plait. It was the fashion for little girls at that time to wear ribbon bows in white or bright colours in their hair. Some of the better-off children had two plaits and two bows, so I did the same. My eldest brother Krishna was much older than me, and was studying at the university. Because Mother and Father were away a great deal he was head of the house, and with six younger children, five girls and one boy, this was a big responsibility. He took it very seriously and was so strict with us that we feared and disliked him. He often hit us very hard if we annoyed him; if the pots and pans were not clean enough, for instance, or if we were untidy. When he came home that day and saw my plaits he fell into a rage. He seized me, and taking a pair of scissors cut off one plait and threw it over the verandah. Crying from shock and distress I ran down to the courtyard and picked up my lovely long plait, still with its ribbon. Now I looked terrible with half my hair cut off close to the scalp.

When Mother came home I ran to show her what he had done and she was angry with Krishna and shouted at him. But he was grown-up and educated and much the cleverest in the family, so he always got the better of her and everyone else. My auntie who was with us at the time said, 'Don't worry, all the girls in Delhi are cutting their hair short now, and I will cut the rest of yours.' But of course it looked dreadful and I had to wear a veil over my head until it grew. Luckily it grew even longer and glossier than before. When he left home and used to visit us, my brother was quite different, kind and gentle even, but it took us some time to trust him. I understand now why he was so strict. Indian parents and older sisters and brothers are very much afraid of their young girls becoming interested in sex and attracting boys, as they may become pregnant before marriage. They think they must stop even innocent little girls of five or seven looking too attractive in case it gives them ideas.

*

It is time I told you about my family. My father and mother were both of the tailoring caste. This is a middling sort of caste with some above us and some below. As you probably know we usually have to marry within the caste, and this is true even in Britain. I believe this custom is dying out amongst some educated people. My parents had ten children, but three died young. The ones who lived were my eldest brother Krishna, my second brother Veejay, and the girls, Sheelah the eldest, then Indira, Prem and Asha in order, with me Sita the youngest girl. When they were first married, my parents were quite well off, but by the time I was born they were poor; I will explain why later. So my mother had to work as well as my father, but because she had been respected in the village she never worked there but preferred to go every day to surrounding villages, sometimes as far as six or seven miles away. Every day she would walk there and back with her sewing machine on her shoulder, unless there was a wedding or some other special occasion when she would stay the night. It would have been dangerous for her to walk back alone in the dark as there were sometimes bad men about who might have attacked her. She was popular with the farmers and their wives for whom she worked, so at these feasts they would give her plenty of food to take home, enough for several days.

I have never heard of any other mother who did so much for her family and loved them all so well. When she was not sewing for other families she would sew for us, making clothes and everything we needed in the house. I never saw her idle, for she would cook and clean and milk the animals and look after the garden. I always wanted to be near her and would sleep near her wherever she was. While she was away I longed for her, sometimes so much that when my sisters or brothers were angry with me I would run out of the house and look for her in the villages, sometimes running for miles. Mother meant everything to us and she took responsibility for everything. As she could not be with us very much she was very firm, even stern, and we were frightened to offend her. We did not resent this for we knew she loved us and wanted our good.

I often wondered how Mother could live with so little sleep. She only lay down on her bed when she was ill, and this did not often happen. Then she would refuse to see a doctor or take any medicine; in spite of this she always recovered quite soon. In the evening when others were resting after a day's work she would sit cross-legged on the floor on her blanket in front of her sewing machine, the light bulb pulled down low over her head so that she could see to work. During the night she would doze off from time to time and her head would drop forward, but she would wake with a jerk and go on sewing. Less often she would sink down onto her blanket and sleep a little. I know just how it was because as usual I slept close to her.

Often there were three or four girls from our street – one rich girl, a friend of Asha's, my next elder sister, and sometimes more girls from around – who would come to spend the evening and perhaps bring their quilts and stay the night. It was Mother who attracted them because she was lively and friendly and stayed up so late while their mothers went early to bed. The girls would bring their books to study when exams were near. Mother would say to them, 'Read aloud to me, then I will know you are really studying.' She would listen as she sewed and one girl after another read from her book.

Sometimes about midnight we would make tea to

refresh ourselves. It was like having a night party and I loved it. If we had no tea or milk I would go with the girls to a neighbour's house and knock on the door to wake them up and shout, 'Open up the shop, we need tea and milk.' Sometimes they would curse and grumble, but we would say, 'Please help us, we have exams tomorrow.' This would make them sorry for us, so someone would take a lantern and go to the shop to sell us the tea and milk. If no one would help us we would do without and boil up some fennel leaves instead. How often later I was to remember those happy times and wonder if girls in the village were still the same.

In the morning Mother would call us early and take each girl to the pump and wake her up properly with the cold water. If there were exams that day we were always given fresh yoghurt just before we left to clear our brains. Mother knew how important it was for us to have a good education and pass our exams. She was sorry she had not had our chances, but in spite of this she was very clever in many ways. She had never learned tailoring but had taught herself to make beautiful clothes; with her machine she did embroidery, inventing all the designs herself, each one different. Watching her I learned to make doll's clothes, and these were so pretty that other girls wanted them too. I had an idea; I went round the village shops and sold them to the girls who worked there. Unfortunately the girls were so tempted by my doll's clothes that they took money from the till to buy them. When Mother heard of this it was the end of my little business. She would not tolerate dishonesty of any kind.

My father was a fully trained tailor and he too worked outside the village, going further afield and staying away for days or even weeks. He would stop in a farmhouse to make clothes and also to teach the women how to use the sewing machine. There he would have his food and not work too hard, but he did not earn much. When he returned home he would often bring nothing but sweets and cakes for the children. Then my poor mother would be very angry. 'Don't take the sweets', she would say, 'they are not good for you, and will only make him think he has done something when he has done nothing.' We could not respect Father much when he left all the burdens to Mother. He did have some excuse for being this way because he had a cousin who had gone to live in Canada and had done very well in business. He had promised my father that he would send for him and employ him so that he too would become wealthy. Waiting for this to happen unsettled my father, but his cousin kept putting it off until eventually he died.

Father would have been a wealthy man himself if he had been more lucky. His father had a good business, a big shop in the town selling groceries of all kinds. His first two sons were much older than Father and they worked in the business with him. The younger brother Ramesh married his cousin Sonia, and she took over the care of my father, bringing him up as her own child. My two uncles were always taking goods and money from the shop for themselves, and this meant the business declined. Uncle Ramesh took enough to educate his sons and marry off his daughters. Very little of it was spent on Father. Aunty Sonia saved up what she could until she had a treasure in gold and silver.

When Grandfather died the shop and the three houses were left, as is the custom, to his sons. Father got one of the houses, the one in which we lived and which is still in the family. Father should have had his share of the shop, too, but my uncles secretly took all the stock of non-perishable items and hid them. Then they closed the shop. Soon after they opened a new shop with all the stock they had taken. My father was still too young to know that they had cheated him and he never had his share. His two brothers prospered while he remained poor.

When Father married my mother, Uncle Ramesh and Aunty Sonia lived nearby. I remember them well. Aunty was old and blind by that time, and as a little girl I was very fond of her. I used to lead her out into the fields to enjoy the open air. She would ask me to pick mustard leaves for her; she would taste each one and tell me which were the best ones to choose. Then she would take a bunch back to her daughter-in-law for her to use in curries.

Aunty knew that when we five daughters were born it was a great worry for our parents and she used to say, 'Cheer up, I will help you. I have money hidden for you.' Mother always hoped she would tell her where it was before she died. She used to look after Aunty very kindly, not only for the money but because she was naturally kind to everyone. They were well off from having the shop and another house in the village, and they lived well. It was hard for us sometimes, for when we had little to eat in the house we could walk past their place and smell the good food they were cooking. All we ever had from Aunty was buttermilk. Each day she would bring a big bowl of it to the gate and call out. Buttermilk is good, but it is so plentiful that the village people even throw it away or wash their hair with it.

When Aunty died I was far away but Mother told me that the treasure remained hidden. Perhaps her daughter-in-law found it. I sometimes wonder if it is still there somewhere, or did she just pretend that she had it? We will never know.

The burdens on our family were very great with seven children to educate and see into marriage. Schooling in India is free only to the very poorest, and though it costs little at the village school it is more at the big high school in the town. All books must be paid for, and the uniform too. My eldest brother who was so clever won scholarships, but he had to be fed and clothed and given pocket money when other young men were earning. Nearly all this came from Mother's work, and what she could not earn she had to borrow, either from relatives or the village moneylender. To pay for five girls to be married is an appalling burden, for without a good dowry there is little chance of a good husband. All marriages in the village were arranged, and much bargaining took place. If there is no money to go with the bride she must bring many fine saris, gold and jewellery, bed quilts and mats, and these days perhaps TV sets, washing machines and other expensive goods. The bridegroom must be given fine clothes at least. Most of all, the wedding feast costs thousands of rupees. My mother worried and worried about these things, which had to be done or else the whole family would be utterly disgraced. This is one reason why girl babies are not welcomed in the family. When a boy is born there is rejoicing. A party is given, sweets presented to all, and there is song and dance. This is not done when a girl is born.

Mother wanted us all to have a good education, even the girls, because although we would certainly be getting married and perhaps never work outside the home, a girl with education is worth more in marriage. This is very important if there is no dowry. Of course, times are changing and it is becoming more usual for women who have had training to work outside the home. My eldest sister Sheelah trained as a teacher; she too was quite clever. Indira learned handicrafts in college; Prem took nurse's training and she too did well; Asha studied to be a secretary. Mother was proud to have educated daughters. She herself had had little opportunity, but she was unusually independent and strong-minded.

There was one special sorrow in our family; the second son Veejay had a terrible accident. It came about this way. Far away in the mountains to the north is the famous shrine of the Maharanee Shiva chert purnee, a goddess with eight arms who sits on a lion. She appeared to some children there long ago as the Virgin Mary appeared to Bernadette in Lourdes. She asked that a shrine be built there in her honour, and there is now a great temple. Many Hindus and others make pilgrimage to pray to her and may stay away for months. My parents went and took my brother Veejay. One day he was riding his bicycle down a steep mountain road when the brakes failed and he ran into a lorry. His back was badly injured and he was in hospital for several years, off and on. He never recovered completely. Like schools, hospitals in India are not free, so Mother had to find the money for treatment and medicines. It made us all very sad to see him an invalid, his career ruined. Even now, when my brother is living in our family house with his wife and children, he is not yet cured. He does odd jobs in the village but he is not well off. Mother never retired; she went on working to repay the debts she had incurred for us children. By the time she died, every one had been paid up, but the sad thing was that she did not live long enough to enjoy her freedom.

*

I went to school in the village when I was about five. We learned to read and write in our local tongue, the language we speak at home, and in the language which is spoken more in the towns. We also did arithmetic and sewing. I did my lessons well and liked being in school. All my older sisters and brothers were clever, though only Krishna went to the university; perhaps I was not as bright as them, but I did well enough, and expected to get a good education. But by the time I was twelve and going to the secondary school things at home changed. Krishna had left and gone to work in Bombay. Prem and Asha were living in hostels in town and studying at college, so I was very much alone, growing up with little help and guidance.

When I was thirteen I started my periods. My friend had told me when it had happened to her, but no one else had ever spoken of it, so I was very much in the dark. It first happened at school and I came home worried and frightened. Mother was home that day and was angry when she saw I had left school. 'Why have you come home like this?' she asked. I did not dare to tell her, but ran upstairs and stayed alone all day. I suppose she guessed but we never spoke of it. I put some cotton stuff in my pants, as there were no sanitary towels in those days, but it was very uncomfortable and blood often came through. This was a great worry to me. I soon found out that a menstruating woman is thought to be unclean and is not welcomed in her neighbours' houses as she will contaminate them. It is thought that food she touches may be poisonous and that she may cast a 'shadow' on children. I found this depressing.

All the same, the first year at secondary school was interesting. We started to learn English and geography and history, and I think that anything I know dates from that time. I loved my English teacher and would visit her in her house and help her, and it seemed I would do well like my brothers and sisters, but something went wrong with me. Looking back, I think I felt very unloved and unvalued at that time, and I also had the idea that I was different from other people. It was not because I believed I was cleverer or more beautiful than other girls, I just felt strange, as if I did not belong where I was. When I went to visit Prem and Asha in their hostel in the town I loved it and longed to stay there. Although it was not allowed, they used to keep me there in secret sometimes. Prem began to work as a nurse in the local hospital and I used to visit her there. Some of the staff were white people, and I had only seen them once before. In fact the first time I saw them it made a deep impression on me. We were in class one day when the teacher told us that some white people were walking along the street, so we stood up on chairs at the windows to look out. A group of young girls, most of them with blonde hair and very fair complexions, were quite near us and we stared at them fascinated. I thought they looked like angels. When I saw the white nurses I was also drawn to them; my one ambition was to become a nurse and wear the uniform and be like them.

A year passed by; I was fourteen, and suddenly my whole life changed. I fell in love. Instead of learning in school I was in a dream all day, and at home I did little but play and try on clothes and do my hair. I told no one, but I could think of little else but a young man called Rama, who had come to the village to live with his aunt, who was one of my cousins. He was much older than I was, about twenty-four, unmarried still, and an engineer working in a neighbouring town. As he was a relative and I knew his sister Vina very well, I had every excuse to go there and see him as often as I wanted. I would go every day just to be near him, listen to him, look at him, and make his tea. While he was away, I would even go up to the room where he slept, to look at his clothes and touch them. I knew nothing about sex, my love was innocent and ideal, but it was very strong, as first love so often is.

Rama was very good-looking, tall, slender and always well dressed in a suit with shirt and tie, European style, and I was impressed with this. He was kind and friendly to me, would tease and laugh at me, and help me with my homework. He must have guessed how I felt about him, because everyone started to notice it, and the talk went round the village. I used to dream that some day he would marry me; the age gap would not be considered too great, and some girls do marry very young. What I did not realise was that he was too closely related to me to be able to marry me, but all the grown-ups would have known. Nobody said anything, yet I knew I should not be behaving this way. I just could not stop myself. Mother was so worried she began to come back early from her work to see what I was doing. She forbade me to

97

go to his house, and when she noticed that I would sit up on the roof for hours in the chance of seeing him she would call me down. It was so strange that she never said anything direct to me. In spite of the love she had for her children she did not know how to talk to them, and this is quite common in Indian families.

Although Mother was always busy and over-worked she was very concerned for our welfare. After Indira had married and gone to England she began to think about a husband for Prem, who was at this time about twenty and had nearly finished her training. My parents had already spent a great deal of money on us: two daughters married at home, Krishna put through university, Veejay treated in hospital, and three of us still to keep, including me still at school. They had heard that there were Indian men in the UK who wanted Indian wives and would not expect a big wedding and a dowry; they would even pay the fare to Britain. Village people think that everyone in the UK is well off, as they hear many stories about those who settle there and come back with lots of money and fine clothes and possessions. No one can starve in Britain; schools and hospitals are free and it all sounds wonderful. In fact as my parents were still in debt it was probably the only way they could marry off Prem. Indira, already in London, could help them. So in due course a husband was found for Prem and she went off in the plane alone to meet his family in London. It was not so very bad for Prem as she spoke good English, knew many British people, and as a trained nurse was able to look after herself.

Prem's marriage seemed to be all right, so then it was Asha's turn. 'Why not do the same for her?' thought Mother. Do not imagine that Mother wanted to part with her girls: it was dreadful for her to send them far away. But the power of the custom to get girls married is so strong it overcomes everything, and you must add to this the mother's fear that in India they would be very poor if they did get a husband. Any man willing to marry a girl with a very small dowry is bound to be poor himself; uneducated, perhaps in bad health and probably with little chance of improving his position. Survival must come first! Asha was my favourite sister, and the nearest to me in age. She would often bring me presents of dresses or ornaments from town, and we were happy in each other's company. I admired her for her cleverness and her good looks, and I thought of her as being very superior to me. The three years difference in age seemed a lot at this time. We were rather alike in appearance in those days, but I felt that I was compared unfavourably with her, and in spite of loving her I was jealous. It is only recently that I have been told by my white friends that I am beautiful, and because of this, as I shall tell later, have become much more confident. At that time I had very little confidence about myself in any way. This may have contributed to my desire for love from Rama, and my obsession with him. It became so marked that Mother must have feared that I might get pregnant by a man I could never marry, and decided to do something drastic to prevent it.

Enquiries had already been made for a husband in Britain suitable for Asha. Indians, particularly the women, keep in touch with a very wide circle of relatives and friends, not only in India, but in Britain and other countries, and there is an endless interest in matchmaking. Mother heard of a family from our area who had a restaurant in London, and one of their sons was in his early twenties and unmarried. She began to negotiate on Asha's behalf, but as my behaviour became more and more worrying she decided that the same young man would do for me instead, and this would get me out of temptation's way. I do not remember that anything was said to me directly, but I heard my family talking of a marriage for me, and when I was quite sure that I was to be sent away I was horrified and heart-broken. I rushed out to Vina's house to see Rama, but learned that he had suddenly gone away. All the village knew that I was to be married and sent away, and Rama had left. Could it be for that reason? I decided I must see him again.

Next day I did a very bold thing. Without telling anyone I took a bus into town and then another to the village where Rama's father and mother lived. It took a long time, but when I arrived I found he was not there. His parents, being relations, were kind to me, gave me a meal and said I must stay the night. Rama was visiting the college in town, they said, and his father agreed to take me to see him next day. And so he did. Rama was playing tennis when we called; he was astonished to see me, and I burst into tears and cried on his shoulder. When we were left alone together for a while he comforted me and promised that he would come to see me in London when I was married. He seemed sad and distressed, and when we said goodbye he took me in his arms and held me tight. I still remember this vividly, and although I was never to see him again, I still love him in my heart.

Winter in the Morning
by Janina Bauman

About the author and the book

Winter in the Morning is Janina Bauman's moving account of her early childhood and the years she spent in the Warsaw Ghetto. Born in Warsaw, Poland in 1928, Janina grew up in a happy, well-off family. But even before the Second World War, Janina had to learn to face rejection and injustice because she was Jewish.

With the outbreak of war, Janina was crowded into the Warsaw Ghetto along with hundreds of thousands of other Polish Jews. Despite terrible hardship, Janina, her mother and sister managed to survive. Many others were not so lucky and Janina tells movingly of their fate.

The Peaceful Years

A patch of early morning sunshine on the pinewood floor, the squeak of a tram fading away around the corner, the monotonous clatter of horse's hooves late at night – these are the most distant memories of my life. The twenties were just turning into the thirties. We lived in Warsaw at 10 Senatorska Street, not far from the district where most Jews lived. Later, when my father became well enough known to start his private surgery, and when my sister Sophie was born, we moved to the centre of the city and lived in a large apartment house at 5 Sienna Street. In its place there now stands the Palace of Culture and Science, the monumental gift of the Soviets to the Polish capital.

I was growing up in a happy family. My father was a doctor and surgeon, dealing with people's kidneys and bladders. My mother's father, Grandad Aleksander, was a doctor too, his fame well established in Warsaw before I was born. My paternal grandfather, whose name was Maks, ran a music shop in the most elegant part of the city, until he went bankrupt. I remember him as a modest old man with plenty of time and warm feelings for myself. Somehow I knew that he and Grandma Viera were poor and dependent on my father, while the other grandparents, who lived in Border Street, were rich. They were rich not only because Grandad Aleksander was a gifted doctor and surgeon but also because Grannie Eva's family was well off. Grannie Eva's family was also the *crème de la crème* of society, great-grandfather serving for years as both head of the Jewish Council and councillor of the City of Warsaw. There were lots of uncles, aunts and cousins on both sides of the family, most of them doctors, others lawyers, engineers or suchlike. Except for my great-grandfather, who died before I was born, no one in my large family spoke Yiddish, wore beards, skullcaps or traditional Jewish gaberdines. Nobody was religious. We were all Polish, born on Polish soil, brought up in the Polish tradition, permeated with the spirit of Polish history and literature. Yet – Jewish at the same time, conscious of being Jewish every minute of our lives.

I asked my father what 'Jew' meant when I was five years old. I don't remember exactly what he answered, but I believe it was very hard for him to explain this, not only to his young child, but also to himself. What I clearly remember, though, is a kind of litany: 'I am a Jew, you see, Mama is a Jewess, you are yourself and your little sister; Uncle Julian is a Jew' . . . 'And Auntie Maria is a Jewess . . .' 'No,' he said, slightly embarrassed, 'Auntie Maria is not, she is a Christian.' Auntie Maria, my favourite aunt, was not in fact my aunt. She had been my mother's and her two younger brothers' nanny when they were children. Now she lived with my grandparents at Border Street, being their housekeeper and a close member of the family.

In our vast flat in Sienna Street, which included father's private surgery, I lived with my parents, Sophie and a maid and a cook. There was always a nanny, or a governess and later a French teacher too. These women came and went, and I loathed them because they stood like an impenetrable wall between myself and my mother. Mother was always busy rushing somewhere, coping with patients, shopping, answering telephone calls, instructing the cook, or in between simply resting, locked in her room. I longed for her incessantly, for a full day spent together, to sleep in her bed, which happened only when I was ill. Of father I saw even less. He worked very hard, leaving for hospital when I was still asleep, receiving his private patients throughout the afternoon, making home calls in the evenings, sometimes late into the night. As far back as I can remember, I lived in terror that my parents might suddenly die. When they spent an evening out, dining at Border Street or going to the cinema, I could never get to sleep, imagining they were already dead and would never come back. Glued to the nursery window, I would watch the quiet, half-lit street until the two familiar shapes emerged from around the corner. Only then could I go back to bed. I never told anybody about my fears or night watches. It was my secret.

For some strange reason I was not sent to school until I was eleven. I was taught at home with six or seven other children by private teacher – at my own house or theirs. Early in May, Sophie and I were sent off 'to the country', as we called the fashionable suburb, Konstancin. In the early thirties Grandad Aleksander had had a large modern villa built there for all the family. Grannie Eva spent all summer at the villa, and other members of the family joined us for days or weeks. Under the loving care of Auntie Maria, who was the heart and soul of the house, Sophie and I would stay there till late September, in accordance with the common belief that the country was good for children. Perhaps this was why we were educated at home, so as not to be bound to the school calendar.

So more than a third of my early life was spent in the big garden bursting with fruit and flowers, in thick woods full of mushrooms, and in the vast fertile fields of the surrounding countryside. Later in life, trapped inside the ghetto walls, hiding in strange, stifling places, or even living as a free adult in postwar Warsaw, I dreamed and daydreamed about all this.

Sometimes Auntie Maria would take me shopping with her to the nearest village. It was a very poor, dirty place inhabited mainly by Jews. I can still remember little children sitting in the dusty road in front of their shabby cottages, playing with used flypapers black with dead flies. Live flies buzzed in their curly black hair, crawled on their filthy arms and legs. The children did not seem to mind. Their fathers were pedlars or poor craftsmen. They had long beards and wore black gaberdines. Their mothers wore untidy wigs. They all spoke a foreign language I could not understand. Their Polish was funny.

The queerness, the strangeness of those people who were Jews like us had puzzled me as long as I could remember. I used to see many of them in the park in Warsaw, but I saw them first of all in my father's surgery. Some of them looked very poor, but some did not. Still, they were all strangers and I felt frightened whenever I had to pass the corridor where they would sit and talk very loudly while waiting for my father to see them.

I feared them, perhaps I slightly despised them as sometimes children do when they meet people who speak in a broken language and look different. But most of all I wondered and wondered how they and we were Jews while other people, as sweet and familiar as Auntie Maria, for example, were not. Obviously it had nothing to do with being poor or rich. There were poor Jews in the village, well off Jews like my family, and Jews far, far richer than us – my uncle Jerzy's in-laws, for instance, who were bankers and wore diamond rings and gold chains when visiting my grandparents.

I learned somehow that Jews could be recognised simply by their looks – dark curly hair, black eyes, high-bridged noses. But this did not work, either. Uncle Jozef was blond, my own eyes were pale green and there were many straight noses in the family. What then?

Maybe it had something to do with the church and religion. Jews did not go to church; we never did. Jews went to synagogue; but we never did, either. Like non-Jewish people we had always had a Christmas tree at home. But unlike them we also had those gorgeous celebrations at my great-grandmother's twice a year. It was called Pesach (Passover) in the spring and Rosh Hashana (Jewish New Year) in the autumn. We all sat at an endless table laid the length of two large rooms, my great-grandmother, half-deaf and cantankerous, at the top, and I – the youngest, since Sophie was too young to take part – next to her. We ate hard-boiled eggs in salt water and matzos if it was Pesach, fish, broth with noodles and lots of sweets. There were candles in the silver candlesticks on the table. I was allowed to drink sweet wine. It was my duty to reassure great-grandmother that the fish was delicious, which was a real ordeal because she could not hear me anyhow. The young uncles and aunts made a lot of commotion, throwing walnuts at each other. That is all I remember.

Were those lovely dinner parties that stopped for ever once great-grandma had died the only reason why we were Jews? And if so, was it worth being Jewish? If I had not been I would have been allowed to walk round the village with a Corpus Christi procession in the summer, wearing a white dress and a wreath. This would certainly have made me far more happy than our 'long table' celebrations.

I knew it was better not to be a Jew. There were posters on the walls in Warsaw saying, 'Don't buy in Jewish shops'. Once in the street I heard a stranger calling another stranger 'you filthy Jew'. When I told my mother about it, she said some people did not like Jews at all. They were anti-Semites, she said. I personally did not know any of them, everybody liked me, I was sure. To be quite certain I asked our Christian maid whether she did nor not. She said yes, of course, she liked me very much. 'Do you like Jews?' I insisted. She seemed taken aback. 'No, not really.' 'Why not?' 'Jews are evil,' she said, 'they murdered our Lord Jesus.' This puzzled and worried me for a while. Jesus was goodness itself – I knew that. Who would have wanted him dead? Certainly not us. Nor would those noisy, dark strangers in my father's waiting room: that was impossible – Jesus lived ages ago when the years were still passing in the opposite direction.

Soon I learnt that it was possible to stop being Jewish. My father had three younger brothers. Vładek was a journalist, Julian a doctor, and Józef, the blond one, an engineer. I was about nine when Vładek was converted to Catholicism, changed his surname and married a Christian girl. The event was widely discussed amongst the relatives. Strangely enough, everybody whispered. I do not remember seeing Vładek often after that, and it was more than two years before we paid our first visit to his little flat where he lived with his non-Jewish wife, Halina, and their new-born son, Jurek.

Lying in bed in my room one night, soon after Vładek was converted, I overheard a sharp argument between my father and Uncle Józef who had come to supper. Father, whom I knew as a quiet, softly spoken man, raised his voice, scolding his brother with unusual fervour.

'Never, never in my life!' I heard him shout. 'Where is your self-respect? Do as you like, but don't come to me for my blessing!'

'And what about Vładek's self-respect?' asked Uncle Józef angrily. 'You went along with his decision, didn't you?'

'I neither approved it nor condemned it. His case is different. He fell in love with Halina, and he didn't want to antagonise her family.'

'Why can't you see *my* reason?' shouted Uncle Józef. 'I am suffocating. I can't carry on like this any longer. Just think how far I could get in life if I were not . . .'

'That's exactly what I hate and despise,' roared my father. 'Decking oneself in borrowed plumes, denying one's own identity, even one's name, just to make things easier, to get further, to carve out for oneself a brilliant career . . . *that's* what I call lack of dignity!'

That night, young as I was, I learned a crucial lesson. Be what you are, never pretend to be somebody else. Be Jewish if you were born a Jew, even if you don't quite understand what it means. Be dignified, don't deny your identity. Eight years later I did. It was not my choice. My life was at stake.

Uncle Józef never became a convert. He died, however, not because he was a Jew but because he was a Polish officer, killed in the Katyń Massacre* together with my father.

In trying to put down the events and feelings of my early life, I do not wish to suggest that I spent my childhood thinking about matters as broad and controversial as what it meant to belong to a large minority within a Catholic nation. I remember those years as a bright, warm time of sensual and emotional exploration, vivid imagination, a growing love for anything of beauty around me; as a time when I read my first books and made my first friendships.

It had been decided since I was born that I would follow in my father's and grandfather's footsteps and become a doctor. I had taken this for granted as long as I could remember. There was, however, a major obstacle to this family daydream. At that time, it was hard for anyone to get into medical studies at Warsaw University – for a Jewish boy or girl it was almost impossible. Though total exclusion had never been introduced in Polish universities, there was none the less a clear unofficial restriction on the number of Jews admitted for

---

*On 13 April 1943 the Germans announced that they had discovered the mass graves of Polish officers in the Katyń forest near Smolensk, western Russia. The Germans identified the corpses as the officers who had been interned by the Russians at the Kozielsk prison camp before April 1940. Subsequent investigation by the International Committee of the Red Cross confirmed that about 14,500 Polish war prisoners – mainly officers of the Polish army – were executed in Katyń in the spring of 1940.

studies, particularly those leading to professional degrees, such as medicine. Practically the only way a Jew could get in was to gain a good certificate from a state high school. But there the same obstacle lurked again: there were severe restrictions on the number of Jewish children admitted to state secondary schools. One had to be truly brilliant and pass the qualifying exams with top marks to be accepted. My father, obsessed with the idea of my becoming a doctor, decided to give me this chance.

So, in June 1938, I sat the state-controlled exams, perhaps the most difficult exams of my life, wishing I could fail and thus escape the ordeal I anticipated. Strangely enough, I passed with the highest marks and was admitted to a state high school for girls in the city.

The summer holidays that year dragged by, bleak and gloomy. I dreaded the autumn. In August, my mother took Sophie and me to Sopot, a seaside spa near Gdańsk. It was my first experience of the sea and I enjoyed it enormously, trying not to think about the future. One day we went to Gdańsk to see this beautiful ancient town which I knew so well from litera-ture and history. To our dismay, all we saw were huge red banners with black swastikas entirely covering the ancient walls. Hundreds and thousands of Nazis in black uniforms and red armbands with swastikas marched up and down the city in time to deafening brass band music, singing their fascist songs. The town roared with the ribald mirth of the future conquerors, while Polish passers-by stared on with awe and hatred. We ran away back to Sopot and never went to Gdańsk again. Yet, the nauseating, sticky feeling of awe and hatred remained.

September came, warm and bright, and there I was in the new school which I had already feared and hated in advance. It was even worse than I had anticipated. I was the only Jewish girl – not just in my form but in the whole gymnasium (the first four years of secondary school). There was another Jewish girl in the lyceum but she was nearly at the end of school. From the very first morning I felt deeply uneasy and throughout the following ten months was more often unhappy than not.

I may be wrong after all these years, but it seems to me now that most of my suffering came from my own mind. The bitter awareness of being unwanted in my form, in the whole school, of being seen by others as different, perhaps worse, and being the only one like that – nobody else in the same situation to be friends with – all this was quite enough to make me feel insecure and profoundly unhappy, even without any open manifestations of hostility.

It was an ordeal to stand still in silence among my classmates – forty-three girls – when they said their prayers at the beginning and end of every school day and crossed themselves after 'amen'. It was agony to stay away from the classroom during religion lessons and have to explain time and again to passing teachers why you were reading a book in the hall instead of toiling together with your classmates. The priest who taught religion was young and kind. He always smiled to me gently if he met me on my way out of the classroom when he was coming in. Once I plucked up my courage and asked him whether I could stay and listen. He said of course I could and seemed rather pleased. After that, I stayed and found the lessons interesting. The Christian faith with all its earthly attributes was an entirely new realm for me, after all. I learnt a lot by just listening and it proved very useful later.

I do not remember having any trouble with the teachers. I was a quiet girl and a good pupil. I believe they rather liked me. Even the maths teacher, a good-looking, vigorous person in her mid-thirties, seemed to be friendly to me, in spite of the fact that I hated maths and was terribly slow at it, often almost giving up. She was our form tutor and met us once or twice a week to

111

talk about matters other than fractions or equations. On one such an occasion, she made a fiery speech to make clear to us that we should not buy our stationery or anything else in Jewish shops. And that we should attend only Christian cinemas instead of pouring money into the pockets of Jewish owners. She even gave us a list with the addresses of cinemas belonging to Christians; to be honest, there were only a few in Warsaw. After that, I could never go to my tutor with any personal problems, though she was still friendly to me.

More than anything and anybody else at school, I loved Polish lessons and the Polish teacher. Mrs Kwaskowska, an elderly woman – or so she seemed to me, though she was only about fifty – was the ideal old-fashioned teacher: very strict, very fair, rarely smiling, highly qualified and experienced both as a scholar and a pedagogue. She would seldom praise her pupils or easily give them high marks. Yet I knew she thought highly of me. She openly praised my essays and often read them aloud to the class. My knowledge of literature, too, was far more advanced than that of any other pupil in my form. I expected a 'very good' mark at the end of the first term. To my bitter disappointment I got only 'good' exactly like eight or ten other girls. Nobody got 'very good', which was not much consolation to me since I knew for certain that in Polish I was better than any of those 'good' girls.

I could not and I still cannot explain this strange incident other than by my being Jewish. I think it went against nationalist feelings to admit that the Polish language and Polish literature could have been mastered by a Jewish child better than by forty-three children with pure Polish blood in their veins. I don't think that Mrs Kwaskowska was simply careful not to antagonise the school or the state educational authorities. I suspect she believed herself that it would be unfair to praise me higher than others. For the first time in my life, I felt myself a victim of real injustice from a person I particularly respected.

But on the whole, my relationships with teachers were of far less importance than those with my classmates. Nearly all of them slipped out of my life and memory entirely after this single year in the state high school. I do not remember their names or faces. I do remember, however, my enemies, my friends and 'the elite' group which was neither hostile nor friendly to me.

Two of my three enemies were big, strong girls, a couple of years older, who sat at the very back of the class. Lacking any abilities or interest in learning, they were now spending their third year in the first form. Later, at the beginning of the war, one of them gave up her education and enjoyed life, going out with German soldiers. For the time being, though, these two blockheads were a nuisance to everybody, but particularly to me, as they took great pleasure in making loud insulting remarks about Jews in my presence. This went on day after day. Some other girls would giggle. Nobody intervened, not even myself. I pretended not to hear. The third enemy was big and strong too. This was only her second year in the first form. She was rather intelligent but wild and unpredictable. She chose me as her main victim and sat just behind me, teasing me during lessons. Her methods were physical rather than verbal. She would pull my plaits, pinch my arms, kick my ankles, tear up my exercise books, brazenly take my small possessions like pens, pencils and rubbers. Physically weak and with no will whatsoever to fight back in the same way, too proud to complain or ask teachers for help, I assumed an air of indifference, pretending – as with the two blockheads – that I did not notice or care. It made her furious. The other girls, at least those sitting near, knew very well what was going on, but neither backed her nor helped me.

The open hostility of my three enemies was far less

painful to me, however, than the aloofness of the bright, serious girls that I would have liked to be my friends. They formed a distinct group and were the leaders of the class, respected by the silent majority as well as by the teachers. Their little circle was closed to me, perhaps because they did not want me to be one of them, or perhaps because I was too proud to make an effort to join them. Our relationships were correct but cool.

I would have been very unhappy indeed had it not been for a number of friendly but very dull girls who toiled over their essays and exercises with little hope of getting even middling marks. As a rule, they would come to me, not to anybody else, to ask for help with their homework. I was only too pleased to offer them this help. And they liked me, really and truly, not just because they needed me. So at least I had somebody to talk to and to spend the breaks with. I was always surrounded by five or six of them. Nobody knew how lonely I really felt.

I can see now that being Jewish was only one reason for my estrangement. I belonged to a well-off professional family while most of my forty-three classmates were workers' or craftsmen's children, some of them very poor. The state high school with its low fees was meant for them, not for me. So I was a double stranger in this school, and deep in my heart I still bear some resentment towards my parents for having sent me there.

The uneasy school year finally came to an end and the last summer holidays of my childhood began. Feeling greatly relieved – for the time being, at least – I was not in a hurry to do my holiday homework for the following September. There was not much to do, anyway. Only the Latin teacher wanted his pupils to work over the summer. I was supposed to learn a Latin poem by heart. The poem was particularly long and unusual. In fact it was a popular Polish song about gypsies enjoying freedom around a camp in the forest, which the teacher himself had translated into Latin. I still remember the

114

first lines, the only ones I bothered to learn:

Ohe sub silva quid longe splendet:
Velitum manus ignem incendit
(At the edge of the forest something shines from afar:
A handful of gypsies start lighting a fire)

My parents decided I was old enough to spend a part of my holidays with them and at the beginning of August took me to a famous spa in Galizia, the south-eastern part of Poland, near Lwów. The events that followed have almost entirely erased the memories of this trip from my mind. I do not remember how I spent my days in the spa or whether I enjoyed them or not. I can only put down on paper the bits I remember and shall never forget.

I decided not to wear plaits any longer, and copying Walt Disney's *Snow White* wore my long hair loose with a ribbon fastened around my head. Apparently because of this change, somebody told me I was a pretty girl, somebody else addressed me as 'Miss'. All this and nature itself brought home to me that I was no longer a child. There, in the spa, I celebrated my thirteenth birthday on 18 August.

With striking clarity, as though it were an unforgettable painting, I remember a small crowd of Galizian Jews sunk in their sunset prayers at the riverside. Their black silhouettes with long beards and huge round fur caps rocked to and fro against the background of the fiery sky; their ominous wailing filled my heart with anxiety and a vague premonition of disaster.

We were going somewhere in somebody's car – it must have been on 24 August – when from the car radio we suddenly heard news of the non-aggression pact between Hitler and Stalin. The next news was that, because of growing tension and the possibility of war, the beginning of the new school year was to be postponed from 1 September till a later date. 'So perhaps I shan't need to learn that damned Latin verse, after all,' I thought with slight relief.

Border Street

The last days of August. Hazy late summer sunshine, trees heavy with ripening fruit, drowsy butterflies stirring over the bright multicoloured asters and dahlias. Blissful silence. Sweet peacefulness.

I am back at Konstancin, reunited with Sophie, ailing Grannie, dear Auntie Maria. Father in the army, somewhere in a Warsaw military hospital. Mother away in our Warsaw flat, to be as near him as possible. He was called up as a reserve officer six days ago and Grandpa Maks phoned to the Spa Hotel with the message. Lots of men spending their holidays in the Spa got the same message on the same day and a true exodus began at once. With little chance to get on the overcrowded train, Father managed to hire a taxi to get to Warsaw as quickly as possible. We all travelled one whole day and night, stopping only to have a hasty meal wherever we could get it. There were queues of cars, wagons and bicycles on the roads; people hurried in all directions driven by the same fears. We drove by quiet fields and woods, passed small villages already stirred by anxiety. Once we stopped in Rawa Ruska, a sordid little town near the Russian border. It was dark, but the narrow streets of the town were swarming with panic-stricken Jews packing their shabby bundles into their shabby carts, wailing in Yiddish. I picked up one word I could understand: '*Krieg*' – war. They were obviously trying to run away – but from whom and where to?

When, in the small hours of that same night, we approached Warsaw, we were stopped for a while by passing troops. Young, perhaps just called up, the soldiers looked sleepy and frightened. They were singing an enthusiastic military song with so little enthusiasm that it sounded sad.

Back in my peaceful Konstancin garden, among loving people and reassuringly familiar objects, I can't help thinking about all this, I can't stop going through the horrors of our journey again and again. I don't know what to do with myself, the time drags by. When I switch on the radio, all I can hear are jolly military marches interrupted now and again by strange, enigmatic announcements like, 'Attention . . . attention . . . approaching . . . Chocolate . . . Chocolate . . . Co-ma six . . . co-ma six . . .' It is frightening. A nauseating anxiety fills my soul. Where is Father, what will happen to him, what will happen to all those other people, those poor panicking Jews, those dismayed young soldiers?

In the garden, in the villa, life seems to go on as usual. Grannie in her armchair suffering from a new wave of pains, Auntie Maria busy with her daily tasks, the gardener, a weatherbeaten old man with a big moustache, telling me off for picking an unripe peach from the tree. But apart from that, no one says much, not even Sophie. We are all waiting. But what for?

About nine o'clock on Friday morning we heard from a radio announcement that war had begun. High in the clear sky we could see planes flying from the west and back. Polish planes, we presumed, but we could not be sure. The tense atmosphere brought about by waiting for the unknown was now suddenly broken. The villa was full of people again, as some relatives came and stayed with us. Stefan and Jadwiga had to cut short their holiday and returned from the mountains, sunburnt, more beautiful than ever. With their arrival, even war ceased to be frightening for me and became a kind of adventure. I decided to keep a diary and got on with it for the first six days of war.

By Saturday, we had learnt these were German, not Polish planes, speeding above us towards Warsaw. The radio now announced, now called off an air raid. Warsaw was being bombarded. We could hear the hollow sounds of distant explosions as well as the spanking noise of the anti-aircraft defence. We could see heavy clouds of smoke darkening the bright September sky.

Towards evening, Mother arrived from Warsaw, pale and distressed. She had been in a raid with Father, whom she had managed to meet for a while. A bomb had gone off quite near. They saw people wounded by the blast. An elderly man was killed. Father insisted she travel back to the villa and stay with us. He looked so handsome in his uniform, she mentioned, and burst into tears.

I knew my father's uniform by sight; it could be admired in his wardrobe among his civilian clothes. There were also two medals, a slightly faded photograph showing Father as a slim, handsome officer in his early twenties, and a bullet shell – all cherished by the family as keepsakes of his military past. Father did not fight in the First World War, he was a medical student then. He joined up as a qualified doctor in 1920 when the Polish Army fought against the Bolsheviks approaching Warsaw. Working for the field hospital, he moved up and down the front line on an armoured train, picking up the wounded. He was wounded himself and almost died of typhus on the same train. That was a long time before he met Mother. Now he was in danger again and had Mother, Sophie and me worrying desperately about him.

Stefan was expecting to be called up any time. He was not an officer, just an ordinary private. In the meantime, glued to the radio, tuning and retuning it from the BBC to Paris, from Paris to Berlin, he was trying hard to make out what was going on. With no career so far but with a sound British education he was the most brilliant and competent member of the family. If only Great Britain and France would declare war against Germany, he kept repeating – we would be saved. This partly came true.

On Sunday afternoon we heard Chamberlain's speech on the BBC, which Stefan interpreted for us, delirious with joy: Great Britain was at war with Germany. And so was France.

On Monday a glamorous car with the initials CD and a tiny British flag pulled up in front of the villa. Three gentlemen and a lady smartly dressed in dark clothes presented Stefan with some documents stating their right to move in with us. They were from the British Embassy which had just been evacuated from the city to Konstancin. The rest of the Embassy staff was allocated to other villas in the vicinity. Far more pleased than put out, we quickly moved downstairs, leaving the upper floor for the strangers. Their presence was reassuring. The powerful British considered our place safe. Cramped in the downstairs rooms, sleeping close to one another, so unusual for us, we felt much safer.

The first thing the strangers did after they had settled down in their rooms, was to ask the gardener to lend them some tools. They went to the garden and dug a deep ditch at the foot of the hillock on which Sophie and I used to play with sand when we were younger. After that, whenever the radio announced an air raid, which happened with increasing frequency on that and the following days, our lodgers rushed downstairs and hid in their ditch. It seemed funny to us. We ourselves stayed put wherever the raid happened to find us. The bombs were not dropping on our suburb, after all.

On Wednesday, 6 September something unexpected happened. Following a telephone call, the embassy people hurriedly packed their belongings and left in their gleaming car. Just before their departure, Stefan, who had already made friends with one of them, asked the reason for this sudden decision. But the British didn't want to say, or perhaps they did not know themselves. They had just received an order to evacuate again.

There was not much time left to think about it all,

because half an hour later Father arrived in his Chevrolet. He looked strikingly handsome and strange in his uniform. He was tense and very hurried. There was no time to enjoy our sudden reunion or ask questions. He had come to take us to Warsaw. While we collected a few basic belongings, he explained briefly what had happened. Konstancin was no longer safe. The German Army was approaching Warsaw. As the capital was ready to fight hard in self-defence, the suburb might be occupied by the enemy and very soon cut off from the city. We did not discuss the matter. We packed in no time at all and left the villa. For ever.

So there we were trying to make our way to Warsaw again. This time Father was at the wheel himself, and Grannie and Sophie were with us. Stefan, driving his own car, accompanied by Jadwiga, Auntie Maria, the cook and the maid, was just behind. The road was crowded with panic-stricken people again, and convoys of vehicles with soldiers and officers were creeping along. They saluted Father and he saluted them, and I watched this with mixed feelings of pride and agony. Grannie and Mother, still mourning grandfather's death, wore black dresses and black veils. We drove very slowly and when I recall this journey now it seems like a funeral.

We arrived in Warsaw just after an air raid and managed to reach Border Street by the time the next one began. Mother decided we would not go to our flat in Sienna Street, but stay with Grannie. Jadwiga did not want to part from Stefan, so she stayed at Border Street too. Father had to rush back to his hospital, despite the raid. Just after he had left and the air raid was over, we heard on the radio the dramatic voice of President Starzyński, the heroic Mayor of Warsaw. He announced that the German Army was approaching the capital, that we were preparing to fight back in defence. Soon after that, another voice ordered all men of military age who had not been called up to leave Warsaw immediately. I do not think he said the government was planning to leave Warsaw the following night; I believe we learned about it much later.

In profound gloom, in the midst of scattered bundles and pieces of furniture which were being moved to accommodate more people in the flat, Stefan was preparing to leave. Jadwiga, pale and grave, no tears in her eyes, busied herself packing his bag with warm socks and sandwiches. Just then Uncle Jerzy phoned to say he was leaving Warsaw in his car, taking his wife, little daughter and parents-in-law. Soon after that Father turned up again. His hospital was to be evacuated by that night. Doctors were ordered to follow the ambulances in their own cars if they had them. They were allowed to take their families. Father came to collect us – Mother, Sophie and me. There was no time for discussion. Without the slightest hesitation mother said, 'No'. She could not possibly leave her dying mother in a besieged town. Father insisted, but with no success. So he decided to take Stefan instead. Then suddenly, Uncle Józef appeared. He also had been ordered to leave Warsaw and contact his unit outside, though he was already called up and in his officer's uniform. Father took him in his car as well. They said goodbye and left. I had an overpowering feeling that I would never see my father again and cried all night.

*

The siege of Warsaw began the following day. The city was under constant artillery fire and was bombarded from the air in the daytime. At the beginning, we all stayed in the flat during the raids. We were now joined by some other people. Mother's deaf-mute uncle came and stayed, so did Jadwiga's father, a middle-aged divorcé, who wanted to be with his daughter now she had decided to stay with us. Then Sister Franciszka arrived. She was a qualified nurse who for years had assisted my grandfather in his operating theatre. Deeply devoted to him and his family, she came to see how we were and quickly made up her mind to stay and take care of Grannie. She was a short, taciturn, matter-of-fact person with a plain face, cropped hair and foreign-sounding voice – she was of German origin. Soon she had assumed command in the household. She managed to acquire a quantity of medical and nursing supplies and organised a first-aid station, employing most of us, Sophie included, in preparing dressings, rolling up bandages and generally assisting her as she attended to all the injured people waiting in the front gateway of our big apartment house.

The streets of Warsaw were full of refugees from small towns and villages who thought they would be safer in the city. Many of them had nowhere to stay and nothing to eat as most of the shops were already empty and closed, if not wrecked by bombs. A lot of people had been injured by falling debris. While Sister Franciszka was busy helping them, Auntie Maria and other women from next-door apartments organised some simple meals for the starving. Most of our neighbours, including those who owned the ground-floor shops, contributed to this enterprise. Everybody had large supplies of food at home: the outbreak of war had not come as a surprise, after all. Auntie Maria, the cook and the maid kept to the kitchen, cooking soups and potatoes in the huge pans lent by Mr Kleinbaum, the owner of a household goods shop downstairs. He also lent them numerous tin bowls and spoons out of his stock. All these were taken down to the gateway and the meals distributed to the queuing strangers by volunteers. I tried to be useful where I could.

On the third day of the siege, Grannie's bed had to be moved into the corridor – it had no windows and seemed safer. Mother was with her all the time. In fact, Grannie was no longer with us: for most of the day she lay sunk in the blessed oblivion of morphia, mercifully administered by Sister Franciszka.

Once, during a morning raid, the explosions came so close that Sister Franciszka ordered us to leave our second-floor flat and run to the cellar, while she stayed alone at Grannie's bedside. We obeyed and left hurriedly, but did not manage to make it to the bottom of the stairs, so crowded was the staircase with homeless people trying to find shelter there. We could not go back either, the stairs being blocked by neighbours from upper floors trying to make their way down. So we all stood there stuck on the stairs. The building was shaking and swaying with explosions, the wailing of diving aircraft pierced our brains. The staircase windowpanes shattered into smithereens and it was dark with smoke and dust. Children were screaming, women moaned. Next to me, a woman clutched her three-year-old boy in her arms, trying to calm him by constantly, almost mechanically repeating, 'Don't cry, my darling, you're safe, your mother is with you.' That woman and her child were both killed by a blast three days later.

While we were all busy giving first aid and meals to strangers, or attending to Grannie's needs, Jadwiga was not with us. She had found something else to do. Dressed in an overall, her thick auburn hair hidden under a scarf, but still looking beautiful, she started a meticulous search through the bookshelves. There were thousands of books in my grandparents' apartment, for they were keen readers and collectors. Stefan, too, had his own collection in his room, which Jadwiga was now occupying. Enthralled by her work, surrounded by piles and piles of books from shelves and bookcases, Jadwiga seemed to pay no attention to the war roaring around her. She looked uncannily self-controlled and for a while I thought that her anguish over Stefan had made her lose her mind. But she was not mad at all. After three or four days of hard work, she asked me to lend her a hand. All the shelves and bookcases were tidy again, only a few books and pamphlets were left piled up next to the dining-room tile stove. I was given the task of tearing them into shreds, while Jadwiga lit a fire and fed the remains to the stove. Puzzled, reluctant, I had a good look through the books before I started destroying them. Some were about Communism, but most dealt with Fascism, Nazi Germany or Hitler himself. One was particularly voluminous. Bound in hard, dark cardboard, its title was *The Brown Book*. It was about the persecution of German Jews and Nazi concentration camps in Germany. It was lavishly illustrated with photographs showing all kinds of atrocities committed by the Nazis. I let myself sink into those documents with horror. Suddenly I realised that everything that Great-Aunt Eugenia had told us two years before was true, even worse. We had not believed her then, but meanwhile *The Brown Book* had been published, my family knew the truth – and had only been keeping me in the dark. I stared at Jadwiga in silence. Calm and competent as usual, she answered my unasked question. I was old enough to know how things were, she said. We could expect the Germans to enter Warsaw any time now. There was little hope that the besieged town would resist the powerful German Army. And when they came we should expect them to interfere in our private lives, search our homes, severely punish us for anything they considered to be against the Nazi regime. That was why we had to get rid of any documents that were critical of their regime. To reassuré me, as well as herself, Jadwiga added that she did not believe the Nazis would deal as severely with us as they had with their own Jews: Poland was a foreign country to them, after all. Moreover, we had powerful allies, England and France. I remember how I hurt my fingers tearing up that hard brown book. It took us a long while to burn it.

On the tenth day of the siege we had to give in and move down to the cellar for good. It was no longer possible to stay in the flat. The raids and the artillery fire had come too close for safety. All windowpanes were already broken, water, electricity and gas cut off.

The vast basement of the house had already been adapted to accommodate a large number of people. The partitions between individual quarters had been demolished, all sorts of lumber thrown away. The only supplies left were coal and potatoes. The space was already tightly packed with sheltering families – people from the flats as well as homeless strangers. They were all squeezed in next to each other on mattresses or bedding laid out on the filthy, cold cellar floor. Yet, somehow, we managed to find a place for our own mattresses. Some of the strangers protested loudly, but eventually they helped us and even tried to make Grannie as comfortable as possible in the circumstances.

So we began our mole's life in the stuffy air, dirt and semi-darkness, relieved only by the light of a few candles; with no water and no hot meals; in full awareness that we might die in a fire or be buried alive under rubble at any moment.

There were all kinds of people camping with us. Jews and non-Jews, people who were well off and people who were poor. Some of them were panic-stricken, some women moaned and screamed. Others were numb with fear or calm and self-controlled. I remember a Mr Bachner, a shopkeeper, who pretended to be quite calm and whenever a particularly heavy explosion seemed to shatter the walls, he just repeated, 'Nothing happened, nothing happened, just one more plant pot dropped down from the window-sill up there.' Nobody laughed at his joke. One old Jew prayed constantly. A young Christian woman whispered her prayers next to him. From time to time people squabbled noisily over two inches of space or access to a candle. But on the whole, we were all understanding and helpful with one another.

Mr Kleinbaum with his wife and two daughters were

squeezed in next to the family of a middle-aged business-man. There was something going on in the darkness between the businessman and Kleinbaum's younger daughter, Lucy, a fleshy twenty-year-old blonde. I could sense rather than see it. I could bet that in the most dangerous moments she drew close to him and he stroked her fair silky hair. Lucy's parents certainly knew it but did not interfere, while the businessman's wife crouched sobbing next to him.

Two boys kept showing off how brave they were. They obviously wanted to impress me, or Jadwiga, or both of us. I found them ridiculous. There was a third boy, though, whom I liked. He sat quietly with his mother on our left, trying to read in the faint candlelight. As I was trying to read by the same candle, we soon became acquainted. His name was Artek and he was just three months my senior. He lived on the second floor, opposite my grandparents' flat. His father had left with the army on the same day as my father. Artek turned out to be a serious, sensitive boy. Not really handsome, but gentle-looking. We talked a lot and made friends at once.

On 25 September – it was Monday, the day of Rosh Hashana, the Jewish New Year – all hell on earth broke loose. We learnt later that it was the final German storming of Warsaw, but squatting in horror amidst the quaking and rocking walls of the basement we thought the Nazis meant to raze the nearby Jewish quarter to the ground, choosing a Jewish holiday to do so. This was true enough. Time stopped, life seemed to be coming to an end, we could only pray to be swallowed up by the inferno quickly and painlessly.

Once in the space of that dark, stagnant time, I was taken by the hand and led through the underground labyrinth up to a deserted ground-floor shop. I was suddenly dazzled by tremendous light, deafened by a mixture of weird sounds – roars, jingles, wheezing. An immense wall of flame stood in front of the shop's broken window: the other side of Border Street was on fire. There was nothing but brightness and sound. We stood in perfect emptiness, Artek and I, out of the human world, on the brink of life. Spellbound we held on to one another tightly. We did not utter a word. Just stayed there enthralled by the flames, for hours and hours, or maybe for a few seconds only, I do not know. Then we kissed, the first kiss of my life and his. And the last – we believed.

The storm went on all that day and the following night. Soon we learnt that the whole of our district was in flames and there was nowhere to escape to. We just waited to die. But suddenly, in the early hours of the night, a complete stranger camping with us in the cellar took command and ordered all the men and younger women to follow him up to the roof. He would not take me, but Artek went, Mother, Jadwiga, Sister Franciszka. They fought the fire from dawn throughout the whole day. There was no water – they just used sand and axes to keep the flames off our house. They succeeded.

So we were all alive when the storm came to an end and ominous silence took the place of a pandemonium of sounds. In this sudden silence we tried to guess at the future. There were the optimists, like Mr Bachner, who believed, or just pretended to believe that the German Army had been defeated by the Allies and that General Sikorski* with his troops had come to the rescue of Warsaw. But most of us were defiant. When, after a time, we ventured out of our shelter to explore the upper floors, a voice reached us from a radio set left surprisingly intact. It was the voice of Major Starzyński, hoarse and breaking as he announced the surrender of Warsaw.

*General Władysław Sikorski was well known for his bravery in the First World War and for his political activity between the two wars. From September 1939 to July 1943 he was Prime Minister and Commander-in-Chief of the Polish Army in exile.

We returned to our flat covered now with thick layers of broken glass, white dust and black soot. Cold draughts roamed freely around the rooms bringing a sharp smell of smouldering ruins. At first, there was no sign of the conquerors in the street, and we did not even think about them. We set to to make our place fit to live in. Our food supplies were already exhausted and somebody had to go out and look for something to eat. Jadwiga found two large baskets – one for herself, the other one for me – and off we went. What we saw I can only describe as a dead town, ruined and burnt to the ground – or so it seemed at first. Many buildings were still smouldering, pavements destroyed, deep bomb craters all around. A few emaciated people could be seen wandering to and fro like us, looking for food. On one occasion, we saw a crowd swarming around a bomb crater, doing something we could not understand until we came close. Deep down in the crater lay the corpse of a horse killed by the bomb. Excited people dived down into the hole with knives or penknives to hack off bits of the horse's flesh. Soon the corpse was opened wide and the plunderers fought over the steaming liver. We retreated, sick with disgust. The incident brought home to us, however, that our search for food was hopeless. On our way back we ventured a walk through Ogród Saski (Saxon Garden), the beautiful eighteenth-century public park where I had played as a young child. It was deserted and peaceful with no signs of devastation. The ancient trees, all gold and scarlet, stood still under the blue sky. Thick layers of dry leaves rustled under our feet as we walked in silence. Then, in the grass, under a horse chestnut tree, we saw lovely glossy, ruddy chestnuts. The lawn was littered with them. I had never seen such a lot of chestnuts before, there had always been a host of children preying on them at other times. Now they were all mine. And Jadwiga's. With mindless joy we began to pick them up and fill our empty baskets to the top. We felt almost happy carrying our useless load back home.

The following day we saw the Germans for the first time. They were marching along Border Street, just beneath our front windows, tall, well fed, neat in ther field-grey uniforms. They sang out loud their *Heili Heilo*, the odious song of evil's victory I had already heard in Gdańsk. This sight and sound marked for me the real beginning of the German occupation.

Behind the Walls

18 April 1941

Two little boys are begging in the street next to our gate. I see them there every time I go out. Or they might be girls, I don't know. Their heads are shaven, clothes in rags, their frightfully emaciated tiny faces bring to mind birds rather than human beings. Their huge black eyes, though, are human; so full of sadness . . . The younger one may be five or six, the older ten perhaps. They don't move, they don't speak. The little one sits on the pavement, the bigger one just stands there with his claw of a hand stretched out. I must remember now to bring them some food whenever I go out. This morning, on my way to lessons, I gave them my bread and butter meant for lunch. They didn't show any excitement or gratitude, just took it from me and began to eat at once. I saw other people giving them bread or some money, too. This keeps them alive. But, my God, what kind of life is it?

On my way to Pawia Street, strewn all along with starving people leaning against the walls or sitting on the pavements, not strong enough to walk, I kept accusing myself of being well fed and for that reason entirely indifferent to their plight. I talked to Hanka and Zula about it after class. 'Don't you think the way we live is highly immoral?' I asked. 'We eat our

breakfast, lunch and supper, we occupy our minds
with the French Revolution or Polish poetry, or just
which one of us L. fancies the most; then we go to bed
with a good novel and peacefully fall asleep. At the
same time they are starving and dying.' 'There's
nothing we can do for them,' said Zula sadly, 'for the
hundreds and thousands of them.' 'Of course not. But
for some of them perhaps? Each of us for somebody?'
'Would you and your family be willing to take home
these two begging boys?' asked Hanka very seriously.
'To share not only food but also beds with them, live
with them for better or worse?'

I had no ready answer to her question, and the more
I think about it now, the clearer I see the answer is
'No'. No point in asking my family, I don't want them
myself. The idea of stopping our lessons and giving the
money we pay for them each month to the poor won't
work either: the teachers who live on it would soon be
reduced to poverty. So what can we do? The only
conclusion we have managed to come to so far is: we
must find a way of being helpful, giving our time,
skills(?), physical strength . . . Yes, but how?

The problem was neither forgotten nor solved. Not for
the time being, anyway. Days passed by, new problems
arose to wonder about or struggle with.

15 May 1941, 2 a.m.
It was – and still is – the worst day of my life. Worse
than the raids, worse than typhus. I can't sleep, I
can't even lie still. I have to wait till the morning when
we'll run back to hospital and learn . . . Mother paces
the room, four steps up and four steps down, her face
blank, her eyes dry, as if she had already run out of
tears. I don't know how to comfort her, so I don't even
try.

For me this all started at noon. I was walking back
from Zula's place deep in thought about maths, the

Polish essay L. wants us to write, and other things like that. When I entered our gate, that Goldberg woman from the third floor was there, very nervous. 'What news? What news?' she shouted when she saw me. 'News about what?' I asked. 'About your sister of course!' Then she realised I knew nothing and told me the story. This morning Sophie was on her way to her classes, as usual. As she was crossing the traffic lane a heavy German lorry, one of the eight-wheel type, knocked her down and drove away at top speed. It happened just in front of Dr Korczak's* Children's Home and some kids saw it from the window. They called the doctor and some other staff. They all ran down and picked up Sophie who lay in the middle of the road, unconscious and spattered with blood.

They somehow managed to get her to hospital (I wonder how, it's a long way, the hospital is at the end of our street). By coincidence a nurse called Sabina, who used to work with Dad, recognised Sophie and sent somebody to fetch Mother. The person said Sophie was still alive. 'Your poor, poor mother,' sobbed Mrs Goldberg, but I didn't stop to listen. I rushed to the hospital. First thing I saw in the hall was Sophie on the stretcher on the floor next to the entrance. She was unconscious and not herself. Her head was tightly bandaged, her face white, her left eyelid enormously swollen. Mother crouched next to the stretcher wiping Sophie's face with a damp sponge. Sister Sabina came and said the doctor who had already seen Sophie suspected her left foot and left eye were seriously damaged. He also said she had concussion. It was too soon to say whether she would survive and if so whether her leg and eye would be saved.

*Janusz Korczak was a doctor, writer, educator and social worker, and the founder and head of an orphanage in the ghetto.

We stayed there in the hall for the rest of the afternoon. There was no spare bed for Sophie. All wards, halls and corridors of the hospital were tightly packed with seriously ill people. But towards the evening Sister Sabina came down, a spark of triumph in her eyes. A patient had just died, she said, and she had used all her influence to keep his bed for Sophie. Stefan, who was on duty, helped Sister Sabina carry the stretcher upstairs. Mother and I followed them to the ward. As we lifted Sophie from the stretcher, she suddenly opened her right eye and stared at us. Then, in bed, she touched her bandaged head, neck and shoulders as if she were searching for something. She didn't find what she was looking for. Her beautiful black silky plaits, her pride, had been cut off first thing in the hospital. To our great amazement, we saw tears streaming – drop, drop – from her healthy eye. It meant she was conscious again. Soon we had to leave since the curfew was approaching. Now we wait.

Same day, 8 p.m.
Sophie is going to live, the doctors say. The concussion is slight, it will heal if she lies still for a week or two. The eye doesn't seem to be damaged inside, either. The worst thing is her foot, both flesh and bones mangled. They might decide to amputate the leg if it shows any signs of gangrene. Poor, poor little Sophie. I've never realised how I loved her. Or what an unusual child she was. My God, she was only nine and a half when the war began. Yet she lived through all the horrors of raids, fire, starvation without a word of complaint, never cried, never panicked, always so calm and silent. I think she understands everything as well as me and better perhaps than some grown-up people who give way to their fears and other instincts we share with animals. Now she lies there, in this awful hospital, crying about her beautiful hair, not in

the least aware that she may be crippled for the rest of her life. Why did it have to happen to her, why not to me?

A young man from Dr Korczak's came over to ask after Sophie. He says the children who saw the accident are positive the German driver did it on purpose, knocked Sophie down because he wanted to. He could easily have avoided it, they say.

Whatever the crisis, however close and inescapable disaster came, we had always had a bit of luck, Mother, myself and Sophie. We did not burn alive, we did not die from typhus, we made our narrow escapes time and again throughout the war. After a couple of weeks Sophie was back with us. Her life was no longer in danger, her sight unimpaired, her foot saved. She was an invalid for no more than six months, during which time she had to have daily massages and exercises for her foot. She learned to walk again. The only souvenir of the accident she kept for ever was a large, thick, ugly scar on her foot.

20 October 1944

So we are still alive. And together. It is so quiet around here and feels so safe that I can hardly believe all our recent past was real. Is the nightmare over? Shall we live like this till the end of the war and finally survive? During the day, when the sun shines in through the tiny square of our window, I think yes, this is it, we've escaped. But when I wake in the middle of the night, terrifying images come back in a torrent, fear creeps over my soul and I can't go back to sleep. Then I start thinking about our present life, how insecure we really are and how far from safety. For *they* are still here, though we don't hear much about them. They are here, ruling over this quiet country, over these people who have taken us in under their roof. And we are here only because *they* have ordered local farmers to shelter the deportees, just as they order them to give part of their livestock to the Third Reich. The Nazis may be losing battles in the west, they may be bleeding to death in the east, but right here they are still in full command. So, any day or night this quiet spell could easily come to an abrupt end. Suppose someone in the village hates Jews, or has a grudge against the family who shelters us, or fancies a reward? I bet the old woman and her sons don't realise who we are. Perhaps they don't even know what a Jew looks like. I hope they won't be shot if the Nazis come to take us; they are only doing what they have been forced to do, after all: sheltering refugees from Warsaw. And that's what we are, refugees from Warsaw.

I know that keeping this diary means taking a great and unnecessary risk; it states in black and white everything we are trying to hide. But I don't want my experiences to sink into oblivion, so I'll keep on writing, if not for posterity's sake, at least for my own. Now I'll bury it deep in the pallet and go to sleep on top of it.

My mother, 1941

Sophie and I
immediately
after the war

People were crammed into the ghetto by force. Thousands of refugees and the already destitute lived in the streets (Photo: Yad Vashem Archives, Jerusalem)

From Deepest Kilburn

by Gail Lewis in 'Truth Dare or Promise'

About the author and the book

The sights, smells and feelings of Gail Lewis' childhood are recreated in *From Deepest Kilburn*. Born in 1951 of an English mother and a Jamaican father, Gail grew up with the variety and richness of two cultures. Saturday's breakfast for Gail meant fried dumpling and egg if at home, or porridge with salt if she was staying with her Nan. Lunch might be pie and mash, and the evening meal ox-tail soup or salt-fish and ackee.

But outside the warmth and love of her own home Gail met prejudice and insults from white children at school and even from her own uncle. At every stage she had to 'prove' herself.

Gail Lewis writes from two perspectives: she lets us see not only how she experienced these incidents as a child, but also her adult understanding of them some years later.

I was born on the 19 July, 1951 in a 'Mother and Baby Home' – the euphemism for an unmarried mothers' home. And, like Billie Holiday, when Mum and Dad got married I was three. I was sent to my (maternal) grandmother for that occasion, so I missed the whole thing, which I'm sure was a real shame, since all of the parties my parents and their friends had – and there seemed to be one nearly every weekend – were fun for us kids too, with endless supplies of bun, crisps, R Whites and ginger beer (home-made of course).

That was also when I was first exposed to what I now know as the 'contradiction between race and gender', but then it was just the trouble between Mum and Dad.

The first home I remember was a basement flat at number 61 Granville Road, Kilburn. We lived there until 1960 and so my memories of the 1950s are split between that house and that of my Mum's mum who lived in Harrow on a late-twenties council estate. It was one of those new estates which was part of the spate of house-building in the inter-war period which was to provide a lot of working-class people in the north-west London suburbs with their first decent housing.

My Nan's house was on the back of the main rail line that ran from Euston up to the north of England and Scotland, and the suburban line from Euston to Watford and Elephant and Castle to Watford. Compared to the flat in Granville Road Nan's house was luxury. It had an inside toilet, a separate bathroom, two down and three up, a fairly big garden in the front and an even bigger one out back which ran down to the railway bank. I remember that when I was very small I used to run away terrified when the big trains came by – they were so big and there was so much soot. The soot in fact was a real problem for all the women on that side of the street, since all their nice clean whites which went up like clockwork Monday mornings would get speckled with the stuff. There was an audible sigh of relief when diesel engines became the norm. But while the women may have welcomed the arrival of the cleaner engine, we train-spotters mourned the grandeur of the old steam engines on trains like the Royal Scot which passed every day at about 4.10 p.m.

With rehabilitation and modernisation those houses would still be some of the best family housing publicly provided. But like many such houses they were to suffer the fate of housing department rationalisation and planners' dreams and were demolished in the mid-seventies. For my grandmother this was a very traumatic event since she had lived in the street for all of her married life, most of it in that very house.

The Granville Road flat was completely different. The whole house, a big late-Victorian terrace, was let as a tenement, in a combination of bedsits and two-room flats, to black people, mostly Jamaicans. The house itself was owned by a Polish man who lived with his wife and two sons in Clapham. My Dad had lived there since his arrival in this country in 1950. How he came to find it I'm not sure, but since he arrived on his own I assume it was through network contacts that operated both here and back in JA. It was, of course, a lonely and tremendously brave thing to do, just to 'dig up' (as they say in JA) and try your chances in the 'mother country', especially for a young man of eighteen with no knowledge of what to expect. It was an act based on complete trust in the propaganda being dished out by the British government and by various British firms and public corporations, and on the need to find employment and a better career than underdeveloped Jamaica could offer. Among other things, he was already qualified in aspects of catering, electrics and carpentry, but it wasn't until the seventies that he became a fully qualified electrician. In some respects I suppose you could say that the de-cision to uproot paid off – he has a house and a skilled job and lives relatively comfortably. But it's not been without

Me, aged six, in Kilburn

its costs: the obstacles to racially mixed marriages, the continual adjustment to the effects of racism on black people's lives and the disappointment that has been woven into the lives of many black people of that generation. They came looking for the rainbow and got abuse, subjugation and disillusionment instead.

My Mum was the only white person who lived in the whole house, a point not unnoticed by me since I often asked her how come she lived there with us when everyone else was black – or brown as I would have said then. As she would later remind me, children can say very painful things.

We had two rooms and a kitchen, with our own outside toilet at the end of the air-raid shelter. We had no bathroom at all in the whole house but there were public baths and a laundry at the end of the road so we would have our weekly bath there, and in the week have a full wash-down in the sink. We children were always told to emphasise the 'full' of the wash lest people think we were dirty, and given that most white people thought all black people were dirty it was a counter to any racialist-type thoughts that people might be harbouring. This may seem pretty elaborate when you consider that this was the situation for most people in the street and that the white working class had a tradition of 'proving' their cleanliness too. But it's illustrative of the way in which 'race' and prejudice serve to fracture the working class and make for an inability to share common experiences. In this case there was a kind of cleanliness chart, and we black people and Mum were aiming to be at the top. Dad had an advantage in this because he could get a bath every day at his work. He worked alternate night and day shifts then, in a Godfrey Davis tyre-remoulding factory somewhere off the North Circular Road. All the workers were entitled to a shower because they used to stink of the rubber so much. Even so I can remember Dad's clothes smelling of rubber all the time, despite the fact that all of our clothes and bed linen was sent weekly to the White Knight Laundry across the road.

The entire house was infested with mice which meant that everybody was in constant battle against their droppings and their smell. Needless to say the mice won in the long run, especially in terms of their smell, and even now just thinking about mice I can smell them. Still, overall we thought ourselves lucky because a lot of other houses in the street had rats as well as mice, which was much worse because at least mice don't bite or nibble at human feet! Even so I was determined not to let any slipaway rat or too-big-for-its-boots mouse come and try my feet for dinner, which meant that going to sleep was difficult; I always had to ensure that my feet were at least ten inches inside the very firmly tucked-in sheets and blankets. Despite these precautions I was always convinced that one day I'd find a mouse in my bed and that added to my perpetual fear of night-time. I remember once seeing a mouse run down the disused but open fireplace into the front room and I immediately went into that slow-motion vision that comes with a combination of disbelief, fear and loathing. I slept in the front room on the studio-couch, which meant I felt even more vulnerable, but sometimes I got lucky and was able to sleep with Mum in her and Dad's room.

Apart from our outside toilet there was another indoor one which was to be shared by everybody else. This was on the first-floor landing and opened on to the shared first-floor kitchen. The kitchen itself was just a part of the landing; there was a sink, a cold tap and a cooker. I can only remember the name of one adult on that floor – Uncle Lester – but I know that he and his wife lived in one room and someone else lived in the other room on that floor.

On the second floor lived Pearl and Clarence and their children. The eldest was Jimmy, who was one of my best friends. They had two rooms in which the five of them lived. One of the rooms served as their kitchen-cum-overspill bedroom; the other was living room and bedroom. But despite the overcrowding I liked it up in that part of the house because it was always sunny and bright.

At the very top lived Aunt May May and Uncle Stickey. They were absolutely my favourites and Stickey was a great hit with the white kids in the street. Looking back I realise that it was that peculiar kind of liking which white children sometimes display for black adults: patronising, superior and chauvinistic – the kind of liking that a six-year-old Shirley Temple would have for the black 'boy' or nanny in whose care she was.

Miss May May was a gentle, kind woman, who combed my hair beautifully without hurting a bit. So it was to her I'd rather go when I was sent upstairs to get my hair combed and oiled and plaited – that is, if I didn't manage to get away with not having it done at all. Hair was to prove a major problem in my life until 1970 when I ceremoniously and proudly went and had my hair cut to a short natural 'afro', never to have another hot comb or relaxer in it again. At this age, however, my 'problem' with it centred on my fear of having it combed; the fact that my Mum was too easily persuaded to let me off was in the long run the worst thing she could have done. The fact is, I believe, that only black (African) women really know how to keep black children's hair well and impose the discipline on the child to make sure it's kept combed and plaited regularly. My Mum knew it too; that's why she liked me to have May May do it.

May May was also a devout spiritualist, believed strongly in Obeah and frequently went into religious frenzies. Her eyes would roll, and she behaved as if in a fit – it was all a bit frightening, but somehow because it was her I could never feel really frightened because I knew she would never hurt anyone, let alone me.

There was also a variety of other people who lived in the house, for shorter or longer periods. Often it was relatives or friends of us permanents, who used it as a temporary place to stay on arrival until they found their own bedsits or whatever. When they moved they would stay in the Kilburn area or they'd move to the Grove, and some even went to other cities. This was especially true of women who'd train to be nurses or men who were shoemakers or cobblers. I remember a friend of Dad's, who was a cobbler and who moved up to Leicester or Nottingham where he thought he'd get work in the shoe-making industry based in that part of the country. This was a great shame for me since I liked to pop into the shoe-repairing shop he had just round the corner from us, on my way home from school. The machinery fascinated me but most of all I loved the smell of the leather and the rubber. Even now I can't resist putting my nose into a new pair of shoes and inhaling the smell (though it's not like it was in the old days).

For most people though it was into the factories and warehouses along the North Circular, Western Avenue and beyond, or into the National Health Service or London Transport. I can remember at least five people – mostly cousins of mine or Jimmy's – who did this. One was my aunt Verna who came around 1956 to train as a nurse. She was very young when she came, probably eighteen; she came in the winter and the cold was just too unbearable for her. So much so that for a while she thought she wouldn't be able to stay. She did, of course, and eventually got her Nursing Certificate which she took home with her and was able to put to good use back in JA. She endured and survived incredible racism during her course, as she made her contribution to the super-exploited pool of overseas nurses who helped Britain supply 'the best public health service in the world'.

*

Everything seemed to be brown in those days. The shops, the insides of houses, the atmosphere. It was as though the world were sepia-tinted – black and white photographs were just pretend. Occasionally there would be a break in the brownness; the marble tops of Sainsbury's and Home and Colonial, the orange of the United Dairies milk float, the green of the fish and chip shop. But this only served to accentuate the brown of everything else.

Home and Colonial was one of my favourite shops (one of the smaller ironies) simply because of the marble and because they sold Blue Mountain coffee and I loved the smell. My Dad had told me all about the Blue Mountains and how beautiful they were. He obviously associated these with home and had a wallet with an outline of them embossed on the front. Whenever I smelled the coffee I always imagined I was there in those wonderful high slopes, shrouded in the blue mist. Funnily enough, he never actually drank any coffee – he didn't like tea either. This only made sense to me when I grew up and thought about the reasons for Dad's tastes. While a lot of 'tropical' produce was already becoming part of working-class consumption here, it was still completely beyond the reach of working people in the producer countries.

But then the other kids didn't have the delights of chocolate tea, or cane or bun. This was the best thing about people arriving from the Caribbean – they would carry with them some delight or other which was either completely unavailable or far too expensive here. And even mangoes were pretty well unheard of then – though I suppose you got them at shops like Fortnum and Mason's. The best things were the short pieces of cane that took so long to chew but released the sweet, refreshing juice; and the round ball of hard, bitter chocolate was absolutely wonderful since it meant real chocolate tea instead of just Cadbury's or cocoa. It took a long time to make the real thing: grating the chocolate, mixing it with milk and water (often condensed milk), grinding the nutmeg and maybe a little mace, then adding a bay leaf and leaving it to boil. As it was cooking the aroma of the nutmeg would fill the house. When I rediscovered chocolate tea it was from the smell. I immediately remembered it, and it was the first time I'd had chocolate tea in years.

This chocolate drink was very different from the kind we used to get at the nursery every morning. This was always nice but very mild and sickly compared to what we had at home, and there was always a faint taste of plastic that you get when you drink out of those early pre-space age plastic cups.

The difference between the Jamaican and English aspects of my life at that time often revolved around food. Saturdays really exemplified it. Saturday-morning breakfast would usually be fried dumpling and egg or saltfish fritters, sometimes sardine. If it was at my Nan's it would be cornflakes or porridge, the Scottish way, with salt – my Grandad was from Edinburgh. Then for Saturday dinnertime (lunch) my Mum would let me go and have pie, mash and liquor at the pie and mash shop. She would give me a shilling and I would go off and eat this very English working-class food sitting on a wooden bench at a marble table. I was the only black person in the shop. Now when I pass one of the few pie and mash shops still left in London and see that green, slimy-looking liquor I really wonder how I ever came to eat it, but it still serves to remind me of my roots. Dinner in the evening would be either saltfish and ackee (still one of my favourite meals); home-made oxtail or pea soup, or maybe pigs' trotters and rice.

This stark difference would be replayed throughout the week, with English dinner at nursery or school and something more Jamaican in the evening. At my Nan's, of course, it was English all the time (although there may have been Scottish variations of which I was unaware). In particular I remember the high tea on Sundays – bread, celery, tomatoes, ham, prawns, perhaps some mussels or cockles, eggs, and of course salad cream. Occasionally Nan would cut up an avocado pear that my Dad might have given her if he'd managed to get some down at the Shepherd's Bush market. Another thing that reminds me of the 'old days' is horse-drawn carts. That's because the milkman would do his round with a horse-drawn carriage; he and his weekend helper would sit at the front. The milkman's horse was called Ginger and it was a huge great orange-coloured horse that would take lumps of sugar from you if you were brave enough to offer them. I was always too frightened to do that but I did eventually pluck up enough courage to stroke him, taking great care not to go too close to his back legs – I'd been told that if you do, horses have a tendency to kick you. Being very much a city girl I had no idea whether this was true or not, but I sure as hell wasn't going to risk finding out the hard way. But it was really nice on weekend days to lie in bed and hear the clip-clop of Ginger's hooves on the cobbled street. On Sundays he would have to compete with the brass band of the Salvation Army that came to save our souls.

Apart from the delicious milk that we used to get from the milkman (milk is still one of my favourite drinks, only now I'm always told how bad it is for me while then we were always told how good it was for us – a dreadful burden for those kids who hated it but were forced to drink their third of a pint every weekday morning), we also got wonderful little bottles of orange squash. Saturdays and Sundays we had these delivered for the kids in the house, which was a great treat. Jimmy and I used to play at putting our lips inside the wide tops to see who could get furthest down the neck of the bottle. One day the inevitable happened and I got my lips stuck in the bottle. I was scared, my Mum was scared, everybody was scared, but people were also laughing at this spectacle of me walking around with a bottle hanging from my mouth. It was awful and I was getting madder and madder that people could find my misfortune so hilarious. After a little while the bottle slipped off of its own accord to leave one swollen-lipped petulant little girl to sulk in the corner.

The most wonderful orange we got was the NHS concentrated type that came in medicine bottles. I was given a spoonful of this each morning along with my cod-liver oil, which was never as bad in my eyes as everyone else seemd to think. It was in asking how there was such a difference between the kinds of orange juice that I learned that a really ripe orange could be green, or at least greeny-orange, and not the bright orange of the kind we got here. I couldn't imagine a green orange – a contradiction in terms – but then there was lots I couldn't imagine about JA. So I just used it as a way to trump the other kids at school in a geography lesson or something.

*

School was a dismal affair until I was about ten years old. Apart from nursery school, which I loved and which I attended free after my parents had (on appeal) passed a means test, my very first infants' school was in Harrow. This was because of my mother's concern that I get as 'good' an education as possible and be free from the harrassment of bullies. At least these were the reasons she gave, but I can't help feeling that there was at least a hint of suburban working-class snobbery against London working-class culture. Anyway, because of this I went to live at Nan's for about a year and started school there. There are only four things I can remember about that school: playing the violin; doing English country dancing; being in the remedial reading class and constantly being asked why I was 'brown' and did it come off.

I can't remember a single thing about the process of my being classified remedial for reading purposes, but no doubt there was some more or less arbitrary system of identifying me as 'a slow learner' or below my 'reading age'. I do know reading *was* hard. I also know that the books we learned from weren't much inspiration. *Janet and John* was full of blonde kids and Janet was about the biggest sissy I'd ever come across: definitely not much of a model – she neither looked like me nor acted like me! None of this was helped by the fact that at my first primary school I remember what seemed like hours and hours of being read *Uncle Tom's Cabin*, which only made me retreat from the written word even more, because if black people on paper were pathetic, miserable, powerless and infantile 'creatures', worthy only of white paternalism and moral vindication, then I'd stick to the black people I knew. And anyway, being able to read well didn't protect me from racialist insults from the other kids, so I concentrated on the things which would – sports and being able to fight: the latter because if push came to shove at least you'd have a chance, and if you got a reputation for being hard then you got fewer threats; and sport because you could compete against the white kids and win *and* still get some recognition from the school. It fed every stereotype we were being dished up, but this didn't occur to me, nor did I care because stereotypes didn't alter the glory.

I eventually learned to read at the age of ten on my grandmother's back doorstep, thanks to her tireless efforts and the skill and patience of one particular teacher in my second primary school. I remain convinced that it was because he was Welsh, with English as his second language, that he became the first teacher with whom I had any empathy. He taught me that if these words we were reading didn't speak to us, then being able to decipher them was the key to finding words that did. It is of course a search that still continues.

I eventually had to leave my infants' school because my mother's brother, who still lived at home, objected to me being there. I remember this as a simple question of prejudice on his part – what about his friends who came to the house, what about his girlfriends, what would they *think*? While this may be the distortion which comes from childhood memory, race definitely had something to do with it, because my Mum had to come up to Harrow to 'discuss' the issue with the family. Inevitably my uncle got his way, with only Nan objecting.

It was a foggy November evening (they definitely don't have those like they used to) when my Mum came to collect me and take me home. The whole event had happened very quickly so it was the middle of term when I abruptly left this school. Mum came from work and we had some tea and then set off for the Bakerloo line (the one which ran at the bottom of the garden) back to

Kilburn. My Nan came out into the street with us and she and Mum spoke about it all for a while. It was one of those moments that seems forever to occupy a huge space in the mind. I think that's why I can remember it so clearly. It was also the first real incidence that I can remember of racialism within my family, directed at us; or rather, it was the first that I was aware of as a racial incident.

In the street, I remember Mum saying: 'It's all right Mum, I know Alec will always get his way over me but I don't blame you', and my poor Nan feeling helpless and crying and no doubt somewhere inside her resenting the fact that as the 'woman of the house' she ultimately had no say over how this little situation was resolved. Her husband and her son had decided the matter. It was, then, also my first remembered lesson in the power of men over women.

For Mum it was just another painful incident in a long chain of rejections by her family because of her relationships with black people. Her father was always at the fore of these incidents and for her this must have seemed like a replaying of his refusal to allow her to come home when she was pregnant with me, even though she was quite literally homeless.

I was sad not because of school, or my uncle, or my Grandad, since I didn't really like any of them. But I was very, very sad because my Mum was, and also because I was leaving my Nan, whom I loved (and love) as much as my Mum.

Despite this we had a nice ride home, with Mum all the way trying 'to make it up to me' as though what had happened was her fault. She promised me that the new school wouldn't be too bad; that I'd make new friends, and I'd see her every day (hooray!). Of course I'd still be able to see Nan, which I used to do often both because my Mum would go to the garden to sunbathe and because I'd get on the train myself when I got a bit older and go and see her myself. It's a sign of how quite well off we were that both houses had phones, so I'd ring Nan first and she'd meet me at the station.

When we got home there was a big mug of chocolate or Horlicks and lots of reassurance and love. Next day Mum arranged for me to go to the local infants' school, which I would attend for two and a half terms. Two days later I started the new school – Carlton Vale Infants. Mum took me there that day, going into work late for the second time in a week, for which she could easily have lost her job.

We started out at about 8.45 since the school was only about five minutes away. The first things to greet us as we rounded the corner into Carlton Vale were shouts of 'nigger' and 'nigger lover' from two adolescent boys. Mum gripped my hand tight and shouted something back, and I remember feeling the anger and anguish she was feeling. No doubt one thing that crossed her mind was the thought that her brother was implicated in all this. Who could blame her?

I hated Carlton Vale Infants (now the Carlton Centre) and my sole memory of the place is my standing in the corner of the playground at breaktime and crying, feeling wretched and sorry for myself. I left two terms later to go to Kilburn Park Primary, the school of the endless *Uncle Tom's Cabin* and sports.

As Once in May
by Antonia White

About the author and the book

Antonia White, real name Eirene (pronounced Irene), was born in 1899, the only Child of Cecil Botting and Christine White. She grew up in a family that liked to think itself well-off in West Kensington, London, sharing her time between the refined company of her parents and the more down-to-earth company of the servants.

As an only child Antonia had long stretches of time on her own and she filled these by creating a rich fantasy world. Writing *As Once in May* in her seventies, Antonia managed to create that child's way of thinking and looking, remembering what it was like to learn to read and the sort of games she played with her toys.

I think one reason why everything came into focus when I was four was that by then I could read and write. I do not know when my mother gave me my first lessons from that classic primer *Reading without Tears*. I know that they took place in the drawing-room and I can still see the book in its blue and gold cover and the hyphenated words and little black and white drawings on its yellow pages. It more than justified its title, for I learnt to read so quickly and pleasurably that there seemed to be hardly any transition between being able to decipher 'The cat sat on the mat' and finding myself literate. Another primer helped me to learn quickly: the enamelled tin advertisements on the omnibuses. My mother sometimes took me shopping with her in Kensington High Street or, as an occasional treat, to Kensington Gardens. The journey in the green, horse-drawn omnibus gave me a wonderful opportunity to exercise my new skill by deciphering the names of various commodities such as Monkey Brand, Sapolio, Van Houten's Cocoa and Mazawattee Tea. I developed strong feelings for or against certain goods, depending sometimes on their names, sometimes on the pictures and trademarks associated with them. I would gladly have obeyed the injunction 'Always use Sapolio' because Sapolio was such a beautiful word, unlike Mazawattee which I thought both silly and ugly and, for some reason, rather vulgar, perhaps because it rhymed with 'potty'. The one I disliked most was Mellin's Food which had a personal and embarrassing significance for me. The first time I spelt it out, my mother informed me that I had been reared on it and added with a smile: 'I think you're quite a good advertisement for Mellin's Food.' The bus was crowded and though my mother's high-pitched voice was soft, it was a voice that carried. Several passengers stared and grinned at me. I turned hot with shame because I thought they were identifying me with the bloated baby in the picture. Ever afterwards, if we travelled in a bus

157

containing a Mellin's Food advertisement, I averted my eyes from it. Naturally my favourite was Nestlé's Milk with its Louis Wain cats, the fat contented one and the poor lean ginger one. I was never tired of looking at the pictures and reading the story which ended so happily with the thin one becoming as fat as the white one after he had persuaded his owners to give him rich, full-cream Nestlé's instead of skim milk.

The legend under the little-curly-haired boy blowing soap bubbles who advertised Pear's Soap presented a problem. It said 'Matchless for the complexion'. I had not realised before that Pear's was the only soap that had no matches in it and thought how much safer it must be than the kind we used at home. For a long time I supposed that the burning sensation when soap got in my eyes was due to the matches in it.

Although my mother's nickname for me was Madam Why-Why, I was often too proud to ask questions and preferred to puzzle out my own interpretations of a word rather than show my ignorance. Very often, as in the case of 'matchless', I caused myself a great deal of unnecessary anxiety but I did at least exercise my mind. By the time I was four, I was a confirmed bookworm and, in some ways, I suppose, precocious. Being the only child in a house full of grown-up people and having no companions of my own age, I had so much time, whether alone or in the company of my elders, to reflect on everything I saw and heard and read that my brain developed a good deal ahead of the rest of me. In feelings and behaviour I was still a child and very conscious of my utter dependence on the adults who ruled my life but in my mind, apart from lack of knowledge and experience, I think I was very little different at four from what I am now, over seventy years later. At any rate if I reached the 'age of reason' before the official age of seven, I doubt if I am any more rational now than I was then.

Now that I could read, my own life often seemed

depressingly uneventful. I could, and did, pretend to be many people other than myself, some out of books, some of my own invention. I acted out a great many dramas alone in my nursery, with a supporting cast of dolls and toy animals who were also transformed into different characters. As they could not talk, I had to act their parts as well as my own. But the imaginary adventures in which I involved them and myself, however exciting, were not the same as real ones. However thoroughly I threw myself into my various rôles, I knew that I was only *pretending* to be a witch or a princess or a shipwrecked mariner. The nursery door had only to open and some grown-up voice say: 'Come and wash your hands' or announce that it was time to get ready for my walk, or worse still, bed – 'Come along now, don't dawdle', and once again I was just Eirene, involved in a life I had no power to change.

Nevertheless, I did not always want to change it. Very often I was quite satisfied with it as it was. If in bored or rebellious moments I sometimes thought of running away from home, as children so often did in books, I always ended by deciding not to, at any rate not just yet. When Daddy was not being stern, I could not imagine a nicer father, and though I would have preferred Aunt Edith for a mother, my own could be very pleasant when she liked and I could overlook many of her irritating ways when I remembered that she had given me Mr Dash. And I should miss Bessie the cook and Millie the house-maid, both of whom were very kind to me, and our tabby cat Sunny. Even if Sunny sometimes scratched me and strongly objected to being put in a doll's cradle, with a handkerchief tied round his head to impersonate the wolf in Red Riding Hood, I loved him dearly because he was a real live animal. However, he usually eluded capture when I tried to carry him off from the kitchen premises where he lived and imprison him in the nursery. Even when I succeeded, the moment someone opened the door he escaped with unflattering speed back to his own territory in the basement and the only two members of the household to whom he was really attached, Bessie and Millie. I knew that I would never be able to persuade Sunny to accompany me on my travels in search of adventure, though he would have been a great asset, for he was as expert a mouser as Dick Whittington's cat. Of course I should take Mr Dash with me. He had been my inseparable companion ever since the day he arrived and I loved him more than anything in the world.

I had always preferred toy animals to dolls; the few dolls I possessed had no personalities of their own, only the ones I assigned to them in my dramas. Even my biggest and most lifelike one, Cynthia, who had real flaxen hair, could open and shut her brown eyes and be dressed and undressed, ceased to interest me once I had stripped her a few times of her shot-silk frock, lace-edged petticoat and muslin drawers and reclothed her. I admired her looks but I had no personal affection for her. I much preferred a small shabby yellow velvet cat called Tiger Tim who had lost one eye and had a tail. He had started life as a pincushion and was peppered all over with pinpricks but, although ugly, he had an engaging grin and a cheerful nature which had survived many indignities and misfortunes, from being thrown away as rubbish to being clawed and chewed by Sammy who used him as a dummy for mousing practice. Fond as I was of Tiger Tim and of other more presentable animals, I could have borne parting with all of them provided I could keep Mr Dash.

He looked exactly like a real black poodle. His coat was of real fleece and he was perfect in every detail from his top-knot to his tufted tail. When my mother first put him into my arms, I could not believe that this glorious creature was really mine to keep. Assured that he was and that Mummy had brought him all the way from

Paris as a lovely surprise for me, I was too overwhelmed to thank her. I could only clutch him tight and bury my face in his silky fleece.

'Aren't you going to kiss Mummy too? Haven't you missed her all these weeks she's been away?'

I had not even noticed her absence, but I gave her a kiss of passionate gratitude. At that moment I truly loved her. But not as much as the black poodle.

'What's his name, you must name him yourself? As he's a French poodle, you might call him "Toutou".'

I thought it a silly name for so noble a dog, but my mind was a blank and I could only shake my head at that and all the other names she suggested. Finally she produced 'Dash'. I liked that much better. I stroked back his long silky ears and gazed questioningly into his intelligent brown eyes. After a moment I nodded.

'He says yes. Only, please it's *Mister Dash*.'

Later I gave him a Christian name as well, Bruce, after a dog my father had had when he was a little boy and of whom I could never hear enough, either from him or my grandparents. But he only used his full name when he signed letters or official proclamations to his subjects. From the moment he arrived, all dolls and animals accepted him as their rightful ruler and did homage to him.

Naturally he was the principal hero of all my nursery dramas but I never had to invent another personality for him, only speeches noble enough to express his own. His courage was, of course, dauntless but bravery was only one of his superficial qualities. He had other deeper sides to his nature which I respected even more. He was sage and reflective, something of a philosopher, in his way, and always ready with comfort and advice when I was in difficulties. I looked up to him as a being older and wiser than myself with whom I could be more intimate than with any grown-up. Yet for me Mr Dash was always a dog, though a magic one. He was a true familiar, like

Puss-in-Boots, not a fairy prince disguised as a toy black poodle. He had a very noble character and exquisite, slightly formal manners and he always expressed himself in very dignified language, both in speech and writing. Though often gay, he was by nature serious and he had a touch of reflective melancholy in his disposition which made him wonderfully sympathetic when I was in low spirits myself. There were times, especially when we lay awake together in the dark, when Mr Dash confided to me that he too found many problems insoluble and was sometimes overwhelmed by the complexities of life.

Nevertheless, if home seemed dull at times, it had its compensations. And now and then quite exciting things happened to me, such as Father Christmas coming down the chimney and leaving me a pillow-case full of presents. Next time – if Christmas *ever* came again – was any day ever so long in coming? – I might manage to stay awake long enough to catch him and ask him to take me for a ride in his sleigh over the roofs of the houses. Perhaps he would even let me drive the reindeer. If I were not still at 22 Perham Road, West Kensington, London, Middlesex, England, he might not know where to find me.

Tht was our full address and now that I could write I sometimes put the whole of it on the folded pieces of paper directed to Miss Eirene Botting, with a stamp drawn in red pencil which I occasionally slipped among the real letters on the oak chest in the hall so that when my parents opened theirs at breakfast, I too had a letter to read. It took a long time to write out, but it made them look more important as if they came from 'abroad'. 'Abroad' had acquired great prestige for me since Mr Dash had come from there. Occasionally I had real postcards from 'abroad' for my mother's sisters, Auntie Bee and Auntie Connie, whom I had never met, actually lived there in a place called Vienna. Its name had a glamour for me – for some reason I always pictured it as

162

a very smart lady in evening dress dashing off gay tunes on a golden piano – but nothing like the glamour of the name Paris. I had no mental image of Paris. To me it was simply an incantatory word which, when I closed my eyes, I could see flashing in letters of dazzling white light. But Auntie Connie's and Auntie Bee's treasured postcards written in purple ink and adorned with pictures of Easter hares and children dressed like Hansel and Gretel arrived seldom and they were not signed 'Eirene'. Sometimes they came from a fairy or from a character in a book but my most frequent correspondent was Mr Dash. One of his has survived. I found it among my mother's papers after her death. It is inscribed in her own handwriting: 'Written entirely by herself by Eirene aged four.' It reads as follows:

The waves are drifting High alas. Our ship is sinking
Alas now we must die

Yours truely
Bruce Dash esq.

*

Judging by the number of things that I can remember having done or experienced for the first time when I was four, it must have been a crucial age for me. Yet it is only in retrospect that I can appreciate what an eventful year it was and how many new discoveries I made about the world in general and my own in particular in the course of it. At the time, I was far more conscious of the interminably long intervals during which nothing significantly pleasant or unpleasant interrupted the daily routine of my life.

I was usually awake long before Millie, the housemaid, came to get me up. If it was summer, I could while away the time reading in bed, but in winter the night nursery where I now slept alone, except for Mr Dash, in a full-size iron bedstead, was dark. As yet, we had not got electric light, so I had to entertain myself with my own thoughts until Millie came in and lit the gas. The room it illuminated was uninspiring. There was nothing in its décor to amuse or interest a child, not even a picture on the wall. It contained, beside my iron bedstead, a white painted wardrobe and chest-of-drawers that had done duty in other rooms and a straw-seated chair that had also come down in the world because its straw seat was frayed away on one side and was no longer up to a grown-up's weight. Its curtains and wallpaper were equally uninteresting, so much so that I cannot even remember them. I have an impression that the paper was pale, as in all the bedrooms, and that the curtains were of some cotton material whose pattern has faded from repeated washings. The floor was covered with the same yellow straw-matting with a design of green leaves on it that covered the floor of my day nursery and that of the servants' big double bedroom in the basement. By no stretch of the imagination could I glamorise the night-nursery into the bedchamber of a fairy princess.

Having been given what Millie called 'a lick and a promise' in the way of a wash and been dressed in my dull everyday dress and pinafore, I descended the fourteen stairs from my night nursery to the ground floor and went into the dining-room to have breakfast with my parents. Sometimes I was down before them and would amuse myself by looking out of the window. I was not tall enough to see above the stained glass screen but Perham Road was magically transformed by being looked at through it. The screen was composed of small squares of glass of four different colours and according to which square I gazed through the world outside was blue, mauve, pink or yellow. At will I could change the postman's face from a rosy to a jaundiced hue or turn sunlight into moonlight.

However, my father was usually down before me, looking very brisk and fresh in his dark suit and stiff white collar, with his pink cheeks newly shaved and often adorned with a black court-plaster beauty-spot where he had cut himself. My mother was invariably last, and came down to breakfast in a tea-gown, looking languid and sallow, with her soft brown hair sketchily pinned up and not yet arranged in puffs over a 'pompadour'.

When my father had gone off to school, she would ring for Bessie the cook to come up from the kitchen for her 'orders'. Bessie, in her morning dress of pink print, wearing a big white apron, but with no cap, would appear with a block and pencil and stand beside my mother's chair wearing her demure 'upstairs' expression and adding 'Madam' to every sentence as they arranged the day's meals and my mother made out her shopping list. I would avoid Bessie's eye and she mine. My mother little knew that '*Her* giving orders' was one of her best turns in the kitchen and made Millie laugh 'fit to split her sides'. Sometimes I nearly laughed fit to split my own sides when Bessie mimicked my mother's high-pitched voice, exaggerating her drawl and the way she sometimes swallowed her Rs.

'Oh dear! Cook, are we out of b'own sugah again? How agg'avating! You must have been d'eadfully ext'avagant with it.'

To which she would reply in her own character, giving some fantastic reason why it had run out so quickly such as: 'The cat's took to having it on his porridge, Madam.'

'It's the black beetles, Madam. They gets into the tin when my back's turned and helps themselves.'

When her interview with Bessie was over, my mother would retire to her bedroom at the top of the house to finish dressing. Often she would take me upstairs with her and I would play with her possessions while she did her hair, using curling-tongs heated over a spirit lamp to roll the front into sausage curls which were then back-combed and pinned over pads to form puffs. In those days women wore their hair piled up in elaborate coiffures on the top of which they skewered elaborate hats. Only women with very luxuriant, rather coarse hair could build up this structure without an underpinning of pads of some substance like matted wool, called 'rats', or silk-covered wire frames known as 'pompadours'. My mother's hair needed a great deal of building up to achieve the fashionable effect. It was limp and very fine and, when down, barely reached her shoulders. Millie, on her afternoon out, could produce a much more imposing structure without any artificial aids. Her thick mane of hair was so long that, by tilting her head back, she could perform the much-admired feat of sitting on it. I had seen her do it 'for a dare' when there was male company in the kitchen and it was as much of a success with her audience as Bessie's imitations of my mother.

Up in my mother's bedroom, her favourite game with me was to pretend that I was her lady's maid, 'little maid Marie'. I can still smell the smell of scorched paper as she tested the tongs – and occasionally a whiff of scorched hair – mingled with the scent of her *Trèfle-Incarnat* face-powder as I hovered about the dressing-table with its lace doilies and silver-topped jars, offering her hairpins or 'doing her up'. 'Doing her up' was a rather alarming process, for there was a lining as well as the blouse or dress itself furnished with closely spaced hooks and eyes which my small, clumsy fingers usually managed to fasten awry or worse still, pinch 'Madame's' flesh between them so that 'Maid Marie' came in for some genuine scoldings, as well as histrionic ones. I much preferred searching in 'Madame's' jewel-box for 'my diamonds, Marie' (a gold-bar-brooch set with three very small ones) or 'my opals' (her engagement ring mounted with five).

Though I knew that my father slept beside my mother at night in the big brass bedstead, I never thought of the bedroom as anyone's but hers. Millie had made the bed while we were having breakfast so there was no sign of his occupation. All his clothes were kept in his dressing-room next door and his shaving tackle in the bathroom. Outwardly the big bedroom looked fairly tidy, but if one pulled open any drawer in its mahogany furniture, it was stuffed with heterogeneous feminine litter, torn lace scarves, unmended stockings, broken fans, and wilted artificial flowers all jumbled together with articles still fit to wear, so that it was no wonder that my mother took so long dressing. She often had to rummage through drawer after drawer to find the one of a pair of gloves or two matching stockings without holes in them. She was as untidy with her possessions as my father was almost pathologically tidy with his. On the rare occasions I went into his dressing-room – never of course when he was in it but Millie sometimes let me go in with her when she was dusting it – I used to marvel at its immaculate order. Outwardly, there was nothing visible but a trouser-press, a pair of military hair-brushes, two leather boxes, in one of which he kept his studs and in the other starched collars, and a bottle of Jaborandi hair tonic. Even his dressing-gown and slippers were stowed away in the wardrobe, along with a row of suits hung on solid wooden coat-hangers and the shoes and boots stuffed with solid wooden trees, made in three separate sections. If my father was safely out of the house, I would get Millie to open the drawers of the chest-of-drawers and the tall-boy and together we would admire the exquisite neatness of everything, the separate drawers for evening and day shirts, for silk and lisle and woollen socks, for day and evening waistcoats, scarves, gloves, handker-chiefs and even braces and sock suspenders. Sometimes, if she was quite sure the house was empty, Millie would do something very daring which both delighted me and filled me with agonising apprehension. She would take from its shelf my father's opera hat or 'gibus', the most fascinating of all his possessions. It resembled a top hat, except that its crown was of corded silk and had springs inside so that it could be crushed flat and put under a theatre seat. The crown could also be partly bashed down on one side or the other. This concertina effect made Millie look very rakish when she put on the gibus, tilted it over one eyebrow and screwed a penny in her eye as a monocle. But much as I enjoyed it when she announced that she was Vesta Tilley and pranced about the dressing-room singing 'I'm Burlington Bertie from Bow' I was always terrified in case she permanently damaged my father's precious hat. Sometimes she frightened herself too and would exclaim: 'Oh Law, I believe this time I've really been and gone and done it.' But after a little anxious manipulating, the crown would spring up to its full height again with a pop like the opening of a champagne bottle.

If my mother had nothing as fascinating as the gibus, her untidy drawers often offered rich plunder, scraps of ribbon and veiling and all kinds of odds and ends I was allowed to carry off to my nursery to dress up myself and the animals. There were two bits of treasure trove I valued particularly and cherished for years, a pair of silver sequin wings that had once adorned my mother's hair and a piece of cut blue glass, half an inch square, which had once topped a hatpin. With the wings fastened to a brown paper helmet I became a Viking chief and with them tucked into the back of my shoes I became Hermes. As for the blue glass hatpin-top which, for me, was a magnificent sapphire, I put it reverently away in a box. I was quite sure it possessed some kind of magic though I could not guess what kind. It was not until I was getting on for six and Hans Andersen had become my Bible that I decided that my sapphire was nothing less than the most precious jewel in the world – the Philosopher's Stone in the story of that name. It was one of those mysterious stories I could only dimly understand but which fascinated me all the more for that reason. But I grasped enough to realise that the Philosopher's Stone

168

which enabled one to discover the truth was in some strange way a more desirable possession than a magic wishing-ring.

When my mother was at last ready to go out, I too was dressed in my street clothes and went out with her to do the shopping. There is a record of what was obviously my best outdoor ensemble in that memorable summer when I was four. It is a photograph on ivory, very cunningly hand-coloured to look like a genuine miniature and shows my face framed in a vast, very becoming muslin bonnet and my shoulders clad in a pale blue-caped coat. I remember that coat very well, it had tiny flecks of white on its pale blue ground and I was very proud of it. That particular bonnet I cannot recall but I can remember the scratchy feel of starched muslin strings being tied under my chin and the disagreeable noise it made in my ears. However, I am sure I did not object to wearing it, for I was beginning to be interested in clothes and was vain enough to like being seen in my best ones. I had certainly improved in looks in the three years since I had been photographed as a pudgy-faced baby with Socrates. My face had acquired some kind of shape, with a small, but definite cleft chin and my colouring could not have been more Anglo-Saxon and less like my mother's – pink and white cheeks, blue eyes, and a fringe of authentic gold hair covering my forehead. As my grandmother said triumphantly: 'Every inch *Daddy's* girl!'

However, I am sure I was not dressed in my best for the morning shopping round. I know that I detested being dressed for outdoors in winter because of the misery of having my gaiters put on. Buttoning them up was a painful process and, even if Millie was not in a hurry, the button-hook would dig into my chubby legs and occasionally pinch a morsel of flesh into the buttonhole.

I quite enjoyed these almost daily shopping expeditions

with my mother. On the walk to North End Road where most of the shops were, my mother and I relieved the tedium of the streets by travelling through them on horseback. Oddly enough I cannot remember the name of my pony, but my mother's horse was a spirited light chestnut called Cyprian. When we reached North End Road we usually dismounted and left our horses in charge of the groom, after patting them and giving them lumps of sugar. Sometimes if we were having a particularly pleasant ride, we did all the shopping on horseback. But not very often as Cyprian was very temperamental and apt to shy at the traffic.

My father never played 'let's pretend' games with me. It is as impossible to imagine him doing so as to imagine him calling me 'Reeny-ree' or 'Madam Why-Why' as my mother did, but only when we were alone. He had such a loathing of pet names and abbreviations that he could hardly bear to hear my Uncle Howard call his sister 'Chrissy' as he had done all her life. If my uncle asked him 'How's Chrissy?' he would reply firmly: '*Christine* is quite well, thank you.' I suppose that neither of his parents, both of whom were very literal-minded, had ever played such games with him when he was a small boy and that, having no brothers and sisters, no one else had either. Or perhaps his precocious intelligence had developed so fast that, unlike normal children, he had very early found the 'real' world more interesting than any imaginary one. One of the many differences between my parents was that my father was quite incapable of impersonating anybody but himself and always pleaded successfully not to be included in any charade and that my mother, even in ordinary life, was nearly always seeing herself in a part. My father, though very well disposed towards small children, found it so impossible to come down to their level that he might never have been a child himself. My mother, in many ways, remained a child all her life. As a result she got on very well with young children but was not so popular with older ones and still less with adolescents whereas my father was a failure with infants but an outstanding success with 'young people', girls as well as boys.

I suppose my happiest relation with my mother was between the ages of four and seven, before I had grown into a critical little prig of a schoolgirl terrified of the impression she might make on my friends. The prouder I grew of my father, who could not have been a more presentable parent, the more embarrassing I found her refusal to look or behave like other people's mothers. Even as a small child I was critical of her and realised that many other women, besides my grandmother, were critical of her too. All these women who adored my father thought that my mother was unworthy of him and pitied him for having married a capricious, affected, extravagant woman with no sense of wifely duty. I came in for some of the pity too, naturally most of all from my grandmother, but also from others who considered that she was as unsatisfactory as a mother as a wife. As regards my physical needs she was not so much neglectful as sublimely unaware of them. Someone else always had to point out to her that I had outgrown my shoes or needed new underclothes. Nor did she normally devote any time to me except in the mornings. Once luncheon was over she disappeared upstairs to the drawing-room to lie down on the sofa before dressing for the afternoon's calls or bridge-party or, if she had no social engagements, to read her latest Mudie* novel (she averaged nearly one a day) and strum on the piano.

Nevertheless, in her own way she was fond of me and, in mine, I was fond of her. She often took my side against my father, and I sometimes took hers against my grandmother. But our great bond was that we both

* Mudie, the famous lending library.

171

found everyday life very humdrum and longed for exciting things to happen. We longed even more to be very rich so that I could have a real pony and buy all the toys I coveted and she could have a carriage and pair and any amount of exquisite dresses and furs and jewels. In each other's company we went in for orgies of wishful thinking which neither of us would have dared to indulge in in my father's presence. Of course I did not revere her as I did my father but neither was I frightened of her. Though she flew into rages much more often than he did I was never intimidated by them. There was something childish about her sudden bursts of temper so that I sometimes felt a certain superior amusement when she flared up, especially if I was not the target of them. Even if I was, they did not worry me much; I merely waited for them to pass over my head, leaving me undamaged. But if my father was even moderately angry with me, I was miserable till I was restored to favour.

The morning shopping round, if confined to West Kensington, did not tempt either my mother or myself too severely to spend our imaginary wealth. Nevertheless, I sympathised with her for having to part with real golden sovereigns to pay the weekly bills at the dairy and the butcher's and the grocer's when she could have bought far more exciting things with them, even in the North End Road. Some of our local shops had their allurements though not to be compared with those of the big stores in Kensington High Street, Barker's and Derry & Toms. My mother could never pass the florist without gazing longingly into its window.

'It seems such a waste to have to spend money on prosaic things like beef and mutton when one thinks of all the lovely flowers one could buy for the same amount,' she would sigh. I heartily agreed with her, not only as regards beef and mutton, but almost every kind of food except scrambled eggs, sausages, chocolate blanc-mange, treacle tart and, of course, cakes, sweets and ice-cream. It puzzled me that grown-ups who could eat what they liked wasted any money at all on such revolting things as meat and cabbage and milk pudding. However I should not have spent the resulting saving on lilac and mimosa but on toys and books. My twopence a week pocket money bought me one green *Tim Pippin* or one pink volume of *Stead's Books for the Bairns*, neither of which lasted me more than a day. The stationer's shop, Gomms', where I bought them sold quite a number of fat, enticing books in stiff covers at prices well beyond my range – a shilling or more – as well as cheap, but quite attractive toys. There was a fair selection of these at twopence, but not alluring enough to seduce me from the weekly addition to my library. Some of the fourpenny toys might well have seduced me if I had had as much as fourpence to spend but, not having it, I was spared the temptation. Sometimes when my mother took a half-sovereign from her purse to pay for some dull purchase, I would speculate on all the delightful things I could buy at Gomms' if I had had such riches. Ten whole shillings – more than an entire year of my pocket money – represented untold wealth to me. A sovereign was too regal and grown-up for me to aspire to; the limit of my financial ambitions was to possess one of those magical little coins that looked like golden sixpences and could buy as much as twenty silver ones. However the prospect was so unlikely that what I would buy with it was too abstract a speculation to dwell on for long.

I had, of course, my preferences among the West Kensington shops and shopkeepers. I liked Floyd's the dairy as much as I hated Sendall's the butchers. The dairy was cool and pleasant, with its tiled walls representing rural scenes and its china milkmaid in the window with her yoke and pails. On the counter was another interesting piece of sculpture, a china stork with a green china frog in its mouth surmounting a china bowl filled with real cream into which Mrs Floyd would dip one of the graded metal cups hooked over the rim of the bowl and dredge up 'two-penn'orth' or 'four penn'orth' for the humbler customers who came in carrying jugs. Mrs Floyd, presiding over the bowl of cream, always reminded me of the fat white cat in the Nestlé's advertisement. She looked as sleek as if she fed on nothing but cream and she had not only a purring voice but a ribbon round her plump white neck tied in a pussy-cat bow. The pussy-cat bow was fastened with a brooch I greatly admired, an oval gold one with 'Annie' printed on it in little diamonds. I also had a brooch with my name on it but not nearly such an impressive one, a squiggly affair of gold wire which could just be deciphered as 'Eirene'. This brooch was a bone of contention between my parents. It was a christening present from my grandmother and my father was constantly insisting I should wear it and my mother removing it the moment his back was turned.

Both my mother and I hated our weekly call at Sendall's the butcher's. My father frequently grumbled about the quality of our Sunday joint.

'How is it that my mother gets admirable meat from Sendall's and what we get is often hardly edible? At the price he has the impudence to charge for this piece of horseflesh he has the impudence to call beef, it's bare-faced robbery!'

To which my own mother would retort that perhaps he would prefer his mother to do the housekeeping, adding meaningly, 'I'm sure she's much better at dealing with *tradesmen*. After all, it's only natural, isn't it?'

Since I did not yet know that my grandparents had kept a grocer's shop. I was puzzled why this kind of remark always silenced my father. He would frown and clench his heavy jaw, but he stopped complaining about the meat.

The truth was that my mother was as revolted as I was by the sight and smell of raw meat and spent as little time as possible in Sendall's horrible shop with its blood-stained sawdust and, even worse than the flayed carcases, hares and rabbits still with their fur on hung up by their hind legs with tin cups fixed under their noses to catch the garnet drops that still dripped from them. Nothing would have induced her to inspect a joint or piece of steak and prod it as my grandmother did before she ordered it. Without deigning even to look at Mr Sendall in his striped blue apron with his great steel dangling from a leather belt like a sword, she would read out her week's commands from her shopping list, and gathering up her long skirt to avoid the tainted sawdust, sweep out of the shop. As a result, the sirloin or mutton or liver Mr Sendall's errand boy brought round on the wooden tray strapped to his tricycle to the back door of No. 22 Perham Road was always inferior to the meat my grandmother took home in her string bag to 13 Owen Mansions. My grandmother always insisted on carrying her purchases home herself. She had a profound and perhaps professional distrust of errand boys. 'If I take it myself,' she would say, 'at least I can be sure I've got what I paid for.' My mother, needless to say, had everything sent, with the exception of flowers. She had the knack of carrying a sixpenny bunch of daffodils as if she were a royal personage who had been presented with a bouquet.

Beyond Sendall's were two much pleasanter shops, Wilkinson's the chemist's and Evans the jeweller's. Wilkinson's was smaller than Pickard's, the chemists opposite West Kensington station, but my mother preferred it because it stocked perfume and powder as well as drugs. Mr Wilkinson was a gentle, dark-haired man with an air of fragility; he was slightly built and had pale, hollow cheeks and rather sad brown eyes behind rimless glasses. His eyes would brighten when my mother entered the shop. She was, I think, his favourite customer and he delighted in making up special lotions

and face-creams for her. She often preferred to buy his own fresh, light flower scents to the heavier, 'oriental' bouquets such as Phul-Nana and Shem-el-Nessim. On a shelf behind the counter stood a row of stoppered glass jars labelled Lily-of-the-Valley, Rose, Heliotrope, Jockey Club and so on, and Mr Wilkinson would take them down in turn for her to sample. The one she nearly always selected in the end was Night-Scented Stock, which was wonderfully true to the flower and which I have never seen on sale anywhere else. Before he corked up the small medicine bottle into which he decanted it, she would dab a little on her upper lip and mine so that we could inhale the delicious smell and get the reek of the butcher's shop out of our nostrils. The process of sampling scent usually took a long time, but I was quite happy studying the various contents of Mr Wilkinson's shop and watching his thin white hands deftly wrapping up our purchases in pale blue paper and sealing them with red sealing wax from a lighted taper on a little brass stand. Now that I had read *Rosamund and the Purple Jar*,* the great carboys in the window, filled with red, green and purple fluid, in which people in the street were reflected upside-down, inevitably reminded me of the hapless Rosamund. Much as I hated that moral story, as my mother did too, I loved the little old-fashioned book with its brown print and s's that looked like f's which contained it. It had belonged to my mother when she was a little girl and perhaps it had been *her* mother's. In case you do not know the story, Rosamund was a foolish little girl who invariably chose what would give immediate pleasure as opposed to what was solidly useful. She had a priggish elder sister who always did the reverse and a Mamma whom both my mother and myself regarded as a horrible woman. Rosamund took a violent fancy to the purple carboy in a chemist's window. Her Mamma told her that it was a useless object and gave her daughters the choice between the purple jar and a new pair of shoes. The elder sister, of course, chose the new pair of shoes. When Rosamund brought her purple jar home in triumph, she emptied it of what she thought was water, only to find that her jar was no longer purple, but just plain glass. The next time she was taken for a long walk she came home limping for her shoes were too tight. Her Mama told her it was her own fault, since she had chosen a 'foolish bauble' instead of new shoes. Later the girls were offered the choice between a stone plum, so realistic that it deceived the eye, and a housewife. Rosamund of

* A novel by Maria Edgeworth (1767–1849).

177

course chose the plum, but found the pleasure of tricking people soon palled. She and her sister were invited to a desirable party. As they were dressing for it she tore a rent in her party frock. But her Mama refused to let her sister lend her a needle and cotton from her housewife, so poor Rosamund was left weeping at home. As far as I remember she never succeeded in making a 'sensible' choice. My mother and I agreed in profoundly sympathising with Rosamund who was 'idle and wilful' and detesting her elder sister who was so industrious that she 'drew nearly the whole of Mamma's bedroom, in perspective, before breakfast'.

Almost next door to Mr Wilkinson's was Mr Evans the jeweller. Officially we only visited Mr Evans to take a clock or watch to be mended but we often paid him surreptitious visits about which I was told 'not to tell Daddy'. Old Mr Evans was not, as one might have supposed, Welsh but a naturalised German. With his bushy grey hair and busy grey eyebrows, one of which was permanently cocked higher than the other from inserting his mysterious black glass under it, and his black leather apron, Mr Evans always made me think of some old man in a fairy tale, one of those poor but kindly cobblers or wood-cutters who rear an abandoned baby as their own child, never guessing that it is some lost prince or princess. His shop was very dark and his jewels almost invisible in dusty glass cases so that when he produced some sparkling ring or brooch he seemed to have produced it from nowhere, like a conjuror. He spoke English with a guttural accent and it was a great pleasure to him that my mother spoke German. Though I could not understand what they said when they relapsed into German I knew that they were conspiring together. The old man would produce some piece of jewellery, usually a ring, over which she would sigh longingly. And usually, some weeks later, the object had found its way into her jewel case, though she did not wear it in my father's presence. When I was very much older I knew that she filched money from the five pounds a week my father gave her for the housekeeping and, sometimes, I suspect, from money that was intended to be spent on me. My shoes were often too tight for me, like Rosamund's, and my pinafore often concealed a dress that I had grown out of or that was shabby with being worn every weekday for months for I seldom possessed more than two frocks, one for best and one for everyday.

Once we had returned home from our shopping round, I did not usually see my mother again, except at lunch, for the rest of the day. Sometimes, in the afternoon, if she was having tea with one of those intimate female friends who were my honorary 'Aunties', she would take me with her. On 'At Home' days or when it was her turn to entertain her woman's bridge four who met weekly in each other's houses, I was sometimes invited, as I have said earlier, to make a brief appearance, in my best frock, in the drawing-room. But normally I spent the rest of the day, apart from my official 'walk' after lunch accompanied by Bessie or Millie, in the nursery.

The nursery was at the far end of the passage on the ground-floor beyond my father's study. Like the study, it looked out on a high brick wall and the backyard and never got any sunlight, even in summer. Nor had any attempt been made to brighten its gloom with cheerful wallpaper or curtains or to pretty it up in any way when it was allotted to me as a nursery. In fact, nothing could have less resembled the modern idea of a nursery than this room with its chocolate paint and dingy wallpaper furnished with some bits of grown-up furniture that had seen better days. The only picture on the wall was of a pale little girl with large upward-turned blue eyes, mauve lips and smooth ringlets, wearing a white, off the shoulder dress, and clasping her hands in prayer. It was enclosed in an elaborate gilded frame and must have been demoted from the drawing-room. For a long time I assumed it was a portrait of some dead relative as a little girl and it was not till I read *Uncle Tom's Cabin* that I identified her as Little Eva. However, it did not worry me that my nursery was not much more than a glorified box-room. Those cast-off pieces of furniture had the great merit of not having to be treated respectfully: I could regard them as mine to do what I liked with. The shabby old table in the window served all sorts of useful purposes. Turned upside down, it made an excellent raft; draped with an old curtain, it made an excellent tent. In any case, when I was in the nursery, I was usually somewhere else in my mind, either in the setting of the book I was reading or in some imaginary place, so that I spent many hours of a normal day alone in my nursery, reading and writing and acting out dramas with my dolls and toy animals. But there was hardly a day when, weary of my own company, I did not escape down the back-stairs, which were just outside the nursery, into the rich underworld of the kitchen. My parents had no idea how much time I spent down in the basement, in the company of the servants and their visitors. Once my father had gone off to afternoon school and my mother too was safely out of the way, especially in winter when my fireless nursery was very chilly, Mr Dash and I would more often than not descend to the cheerful warmth of the kitchen and sometimes spend the whole afternoon there. Officially, Millie was supposed to bring my tea and supper up to the nursery, but as no one checked up on this, I usually had both in the kitchen with her and Bessie, an arrangement that suited us all much better. Bessie and Millie are much vaguer in my memory than Lawrence and Frances, the cook and housemaid who succeeded them when I was five or six, but they were both very agreeable and I learnt a great many interesting things in their company. They were not sisters, like Lawrence and Frances, but 'best friends' who always took posts together. They were so devoted to each other that, out of uniform, they dressed alike. I remember how delighted they were to receive as a Christmas present from my parents a length of silk apiece to make themselves blouses. I can see those blouses much more clearly than I can see their faces. The silk was pink, with narrow white stripes; hot, vivid pink known then as 'crushed strawberry' but almost the colour Schiaparelli made famous as 'shocking pink'. They had their blouses made up by a dressmaker friend with quantities of ruching, low necks and elaborate flounced sleeves. They were so pleased with the result that they each had their photographs taken in them, wearing their identical cat's eye pendants and their brown hair piled up in immense pompadours.

I found their conversation fascinating, especially when they sometimes forgot my presence and discussed topics never referred to upstairs, such as murder, fatal accidents and ghosts. Sometimes I used to collect items from their talk to liven up a newspaper which I wrote from time to time called *The West Kensington News*. I only remember one of them: 'A cabman had his head bashed in by a lamp-post in Hammersmith.' I suppose I remember it because my mother looked horrified when she read it and asked me where I got such morbid ideas, but my father was rather amused and said it was a good sensational news item.

Listening to stories of women discovered with their throats cut from ear to ear – 'an' they never found out who done it' – of murderers who chopped their victims into little pieces and buried them in the back garden, of burglars who climbed in at night through the windows and strangled people or clubbed them to death if they tried to raise the alarm was deliciously spine-chilling when one was sitting by the kitchen fire eating dripping-toast. But alone in the dark in bed, with only Mr Dash for company, I sometimes wished I had not listened to them so avidly. Quite often I would wake up from a nightmare and be terrified at the sound of footsteps on the stairs outside and at the sight of strange shadows thrown on the frosted pane of the top half of the night-nursery door. The footsteps would go creaking up another flight, the frosted pane would go dark as the gas on the stairs was turned out and I would tell myself, not always with complete conviction, that it was only my father going up to bed. If my parents had ever, as they assured me, been in the habit of looking in to say goodnight to me, they had certainly dropped it by the time I was four. At six, when I was put to bed, my father was still busy with pupils and my mother was usually still out, or, if she was in, playing bridge or entertaining friends.

Without my friends below stairs who included not only Bessie and Millie, but Mrs Bullock the charwoman who came in one day a week to scrub floors and various of their male and female acquaintances whose names I forget, I should have had a much duller time as an only child.

Follow on

The activities that follow are only suggestions of how you might extend your reading into written and oral assignments; you may find that you prefer to tackle some of the talking points as writing activities or vice versa. Whatever approach you adopt, the most important step is to read and enjoy the book.

Her People by Kathleen Dayus

Talking points

- Work in groups of three: one takes the part of Kathleen (Katie), one the part of Frankie and one the part of Mary.

  Kathleen: Mary, do you know why Mum doesn't love me?
  Mary: She does in her funny way.

  Continue the conversation exploring the different points of view.

  Kathleen at eight only sees things as they affect her, and Frankie at ten sees things in a similar way. Mary who is twenty understands more of the pressures on their mother, Polly Dayus, to keep the family clean, clothed and fed.

  Before you start look through *Her People* once again to find evidence for your character's point of view.

183

- Were the 'good old days' so good? Work in pairs and plan a series of questions to put to two different members of Kathleen's family. Use *Her People* to find evidence for your answers. Take it in turns to conduct the interview and answer the questions.

Writing about the book

- What would the neighbours have had to say about the Dayus family? They all lived so close together that everyone must have known everything that went on. Using the names and details from 'Our Yard', choose which neighbour you will be, then talk over any of the incidents that Kathleen relates: the Pig's Pudding, Christmas and its disappointments, or Granny's visit.

- Kathleen Dayus remembers not only the difficulties of her childhood but also the humour and fun. By finding a number of examples and adding your own comments, show how she manages to achieve this bitter-sweet form of story-telling.

Personal writing

- Look back through your photo albums and talk with friends and family about your own 'bitter-sweet' memories. Take any of the following suggestions, or an idea of your own, and write *your* story. Try to include not only what happened, but also how you felt, how people looked and what they said.

  - Christmas, its excitements and disappointments

  - getting a pet, and losing it

  - Granny comes to stay

  - getting into mischief, the fun and the fury.

A London Childhood by Angela Rodaway

Talking points

- Read through *A London Childhood* and list as many clues
  as you can find which tell us that Angela's family were, in
  fact, poor. Working in pairs, imagine you are Angela's
  mother or father talking together with a friend. Angela's
  father has just lost his job — how will they manage?

- Try to work out what Angela means when she says 'we
  were superior to many of our neighbours'. What does her
  mother say is 'snobbish' and what is 'slovenly'?

  Working in groups, imagine you are neighbours of the
  Rodaways. Discuss what you think of the Rodaways and
  the way they live.

Writing about the book

- 'For Angela there was comedy and adventure in even the
  meanest environment.' Write about the ways in which
  Angela's spirit wins through the poverty of her childhood.

- You are to write a feature for a local London newspaper,
  the Islington Gazette, about life there in the 1930s. You
  could conduct this as an interview with Angela Rodaway
  or with one of her family looking back on their past.
  Alternatively write an article using some of the details
  from *A London Childhood*.

Personal writing

- Angela recounts her memories with a light touch and a
  sense of fun. Try your hand at remembering things from
  your own childhood. You could take one idea and consider
  it in some detail, or you could put together a number of
  shorter autobiographical fragments. Angela Rodaway
  remembers the following incidents:

- her earliest memory
- the 'best room' and kitchen
- stealing, and its consequences
- a fishing expedition
- 'making do' – with clothes, stockings, soap and paint
- escapades and adventures
- friends and fights.

Now try recording your own memories.

The Scarlet Thread as told to Rachel Barton

Talking points

- 'Most people here seem to think that we live in shacks in India, all crowded together with everything dirty and wretched about us.' Was this your impression of India before reading Sita's story?

  Write down five statements of what you had thought about India, impressions gained from other people, newspapers and television. Now select from the first chapter five statements about India which were new to you or which surprised you in some way. Share these statements with a partner, comparing your first thoughts with those after reading Sita's story.

- Sita talks about good things from the old days and some of the changes which new machinery and new ways bring. Make a list of some of these changes.

  Work in pairs or small groups, one half supporting the old ways, the other half defending the new ways. Role-play your differing viewpoints.

Writing about the book

- Imagine you have the chance to visit Sita's village and home. Record your impressions, either in a letter you send back home, a travel diary or as a conversation, perhaps with Sita.

- What evidence is there of a close relationship between Sita and her mother? Why do you think Sita's mother is prepared to arrange for her daughter to be sent away to marry someone she has not seen in a far-off land?

Personal writing

- How does your country appear to those who live in other countries? Is it a land of opportunity or a country divided by poverty and unemployment? Write an honest description of your town or village, street and home for someone who has never been there before. Which of your local customs would you choose to comment on?

- 'We're older and we know what is best for you.' Adults often try to point young people in certain directions. Write a conversation between an adult and a young person who are disagreeing over what is best. The disagreement could be over school, friends, work or leisure.

Winter in the Morning by Janina Bauman

Talking points

- What are Janina's thoughts on being Jewish? Note down all the occasions when she talks about being Jewish and what this means for her, both at home and at school.

  In groups, role-play a number of situations where Janina feels an outcast or a victim of injustice, because of her Jewishness.

187

- Janina was only 13 at the outbreak of the Second World War, but she had to grow up quickly to cope with the difficulties of surviving. Look through *Winter in the Morning* and note down occasions which show her developing understanding.

  In pairs, conduct an imaginary interview with Janina to find out how she coped during those difficult days.

Writing about the book

- Write the letter which Janina's mother might send to let a friend or relative know how they are managing now that war has broken out. She would comment not only on how they are coping materially, but also on how she feels about the situation as a whole.

- We see in *Winter in the Morning* some of the diary extracts Janina wrote when she was a teenager. Write some extracts from Janina's diary describing her life before the war.

- Reread the diary entry for 15 May 1941 in which Janina describes how her sister was knocked down by a German lorry. Imagine that you are a police officer investigating the incident. Make a reconstruction of that day. Gather evidence from as many sources as you can, incuding eye-witness accounts from those who saw the accident, and statements from those who nursed Sophie as well as those who were close to her. What might the driver have had to say? What would Sophie have had to say once she had regained consciousness?

Personal writing

- Janina describes the experience of being picked on at school: of being pinched and kicked, and of having her books torn and her pens taken; yet other girls looked on and did nothing. Perhaps you have suffered in the same way? Perhaps you have watched others being picked on because of their race, their religion or their poverty?

Write a story, real or imagined, about such an experience.

From Deepest Kilburn by Gail Lewis

Talking points

- Gail's uncle had her sent away from her Nan's house because of his racial prejudice. What would Gail say to him now she is older and able to speak up for herself?

    Work in pairs, or in a small group if you want to include others in the discussion, such as Gail's Mum or Nan.

- Consider the ways in which Gail copes with racial discrimination.

Writing about the book

- 'They came looking for a rainbow and got abuse, subjugation and disillusionment.' What would Aunt Verna, who came to Britain at the age of eighteen to study for her nursing certificate, have to say about her life here? Write Verna's letter home to Jamaica, giving her comments on such things as the weather, housing, people and food.

Personal writing

- The sights, smells and feelings of Gail Lewis' childhood are recreated in *From Deepest Kilburn*, but she also weaves in an adult understanding of those incidents.

    Try writing about an incident from some time ago which you can now understand years later. Keep the freshness of the memory, but explain its full significance to you now. Here are some suggestions:

189

- a family row

- harsh words

- playground insults

- a friendship breaks up

- feeling rejected.

As Once in May by Antonia White

Talking points

- Working in pairs, imagine you are visitors to 22, Perham Road, perhaps relatives or friends of the family. Discuss what you make of four-year-old Eirene (Antonia), 'The only child in a house full of grown-up people.' You may want to talk about the things she says and does, as well as how she gets on with other people.

- Working in small groups, imagine you are Millie the housemaid and Bessie the cook, together with some of the tradespeople who make deliveries to the house talking downstairs in the kitchen about 'them upstairs'. What do you make of Mr and Mrs Botting and their lifestyle? Are they good employers, good parents, good customers? Look carefully through *As Once in May* to find evidence for your point of view before you start.

Writing about the book

- 'Upstairs Downstairs': Eirene (Antonia) experienced the contrasts of a polite restrained, well-off life with her parents upstairs and 'the rich underworld of the kitchen' with the servants downstairs. Describe two of the meal-times she might have experienced in the same day: breakfast upstairs and supper downstairs. Bring the experiences to life by using details from *As One in May* about the people: the way they look, the way they behave and the way they talk.

● Eirene seems to have had a lot of advantages – a reasonable-sized house, servants and plenty of leisure time. How happy do you think her childhood was? You will need to give examples from the text in order to support your ideas.

Personal writing

● Antonia White takes the smallest of incidents and brings the experience alive by recreating every detail. Try the same approach, jotting down in rough things which come to mind, before shaping your thoughts into a more structured piece of writing. Here are some suggestions to choose from:

– a special toy
What did it look like? What memories do you have of playing with it? Why was it special?

– watching an adult get ready
These mysterious rituals of shaving or putting on make-up fascinate children, who often try some of the lotions and potions on themselves. Write about your memories of watching an adult get ready, or of trying to imitate such adult behaviour yourself.

– shopping expeditions
The shops which interest an adult rarely delight a child, so shopping becomes a tussle with the child wanting to linger in the fascinating shops and hurry away from the boring ones. Write about one such shopping expedition using all the things you remember about shopping as a child – the sights, smells, disagreements as well as the people and the way they talked. You could use this account to make a comment on someone in your family or adult life in general.

Over to you

The purpose of this section is to offer suggestions for research projects, extended study and wider reading.

- 'Sugar and spice and all things nice' is the old saying about girls. Girls are expected to be passive, gentle and well-behaved, yet none of the six authors fits this stereotyped mould. Take two or three of the authors and show, using examples, how they are spirited, adventurous individuals.

- These autobiographical extracts range across countries and cultrures, across time and social class and yet they show many similar concerns. Dilemmas of growing up within families and among friends are explored, often in very different ways. Compare some of these similarities and differences. Comment on how the authors have chosen to write about them.

- People often believe that mothers and daughters have a special relationship, that they automatically love each other. Yet the authors represented here show that this relationship can often be tense and fraught. Kathleen Dayus felt her mother despised her, Antonia White felt her mother distant and uninvolved and Janina Bauman felt she only came really close to her mother through the turmoil of war. Choose two or three of the authors and contrast their different relationships with their mothers.

- Both Gail Lewis, as a black girl, and Janina Bauman, as a Jew, were made to feel outsiders because of their racial identity. Write about the struggle they had to prove themselves within a dominant culture. How do you think this struggle affected them?

- Antonia White and Kathleen Dayus were both growing up in England at the beginning of the twentieth century. Yet their lives were very different. Write about some of the many contrasts between their childhood experiences.

- Although the face of poverty may have changed slightly, it is still with us today. Millions of people rely on Social Security benefits to survive. Find out from your library about any local organizations such as Age Concern, Child Poverty Action Group or Shelter which can give you information about the extent and problem of poverty in your area. Talk to people about the experience of being unemployed, or living on a fixed income. Use all this information to put together a feature article for your local newspaper.

- *The Scarlet Thread* is Sita's story as she told it to another person, Rachel Barton. Choose somebody you know and talk to them about their life. Prepare for this by writing down a number of questions before you interview them. If possible tape-record the conversation. Then, using your notes and the tape-recording write out their life story. You may need to edit their words in order to make an interesting and readable account.

- Find out more about the siege of Warsaw and the Warsaw ghetto, where the number of victims totalled hundreds of thousands. Write the script (or a section of the script) for a radio documentary, giving a history of what happened. Use the evidence from *Winter in the Morning* to construct eye-witness accounts, interviews with survivors and tributes to those who died.

- How did the Second World War affect life in Britain? Although Britain was not invaded as Poland was, many things changed. Men were away fighting, women took over jobs in factories and farms, children were evacuated from the cities and sent to live with families in the country.

  Find out more by looking in your library and by inteviewing people who lived through the war. You could write up your ideas as an exchange of letters, a series of diary extracts, or an article.

- What was it like to be a domestic servant, living in your employer's house and working from early morning to late at night? Find out more from your library about what life was like for servants in Victorian England. Write the script for a radio documentary about life as a servant, which could be along the lines, 'A Day in the Life of . . .'

- 'Autobiographies are always selective and heightened versions of the past. As writers and talkers we choose to record resonant moments, things, places, 'odds and ends' that seem to sum up with amazing clarity whole areas of our lives.' (Brown and Jackson *Varieties of Writing*)

  Take a close look at one autobiography, from this selection or elsewhere (see the list of suggestions in the Further reading section). Show how the author has selected key moments from the past and heightened that experience in the retelling. Explain what new understanding you think the author has arrived at through this process of re-patterning the past.

Further reading

A selection of autobiographical writing by women from around the world:

Maya Angelou, *I know Why the Caged Bird Sings* (Students' Virago/Hutchinson).
> Growing up in the American South of the 1930s, Maya Angelou learned the power of the 'whitefolks' at the other end of town.

Helen Forrester, *Twopence To Cross The Mersey* (Bodley Head). Also published as a play script with photographs and notes (Collins).
> Helen, eldest of seven children, tells the story of her family's decline in fortune, from middle-class comfort to the poverty of Liverpool in the 1930s.

Maura Laverty, *Never No More* (Students' Virago/Hutchinson).
> The story of a young girl growing up with her Gran in a remote Irish village in the early 1900s.

Hsieh Ping Ying, *Autobiography of a Chinese Girl* (Pandora).
> The story of growing up in China at the turn of the century, and the fight against many restrictive customs, such as footbinding.

Margaret Powell, *Below Stairs* (Pan).
> This book records memories of life as a domestic servant.

Huda Shaarawi, *Harem Years: Memoirs of an Egyptian Feminist* (Virago).
   A story of marriage at 13, and life in the enclosed world of the harem.

Sharan Jeet Shan, *In My Own Name* (Women' Press).
   Now living in Britain, Sharan Jeet Shan remembers her childhood in the Punjab.

Kathleen Woodward, *Jipping Street* (Virago).
   Work at 13 allowed Kathleen the chance to escape from the cruel poverty of life in London before the First World War.

Other books of interest

Carol Adams, *Ordinary Lives* (Virago).
   This book contains photographs and source materials of people's lives at the turn of the century. It includes extracts from diaries, letters and magazines.

Elyse Dodgson, *Motherland* (Heinemann Educational).
   A Play about the experiences of the women who came to Britain from the West Indies in the 1950s. The book also contains background notes, photographs and personal testimonies.

Edited by Rhodri Jones, *Growing Up* (Heinemann, One World Series).
   Accounts of growing up by a wide variety of people from a wide variety of backgrounds and countries.

Michael Rosen, *When Did You Last Wash Your Feet?* (Andre Deutsch).
   This collection of poems for older readers covers many aspects of growing up nowadays, including facing up to racial prejudice and coping with the death of a parent.

Students' Virago

The following titles are available in this series:

For fourteen year olds and above

I Know Why the Caged Bird Sings   Maya Angelou
My Love, My Love   Rosa Guy
Never No More   Maura Laverty
Points of Departure   edited by Jane Browne

For sixth form study

The Magic Toyshop   Angela Carter
Smiles and the Millennium   Miranda Miller